A BLOODY VICTORY

Lieutenant Colonel Dan Harvey, now retired, served on operations at home and abroad for forty years, including tours of duty in the Middle East, Africa, the Balkans and South Caucasus, with the UN, EU, NATO PfP and OSCE. He is the author of *Soldiering against Subversion: The Irish Defence Forces and Internal Security During the Troubles, 1969–1998* (2018); *Into Action: Irish Peacekeepers Under Fire, 1960–2014* (2017); and *Soldiers of the Short Grass: A History of the Curragh Camp* (2016).

A BLOODY VICTORY

THE IRISH AT WAR'S END: EUROPE 1945

DAN HARVEY

MERRION
PRESS

First published in 2020 by
Merrion Press
10 George's Street
Newbridge
Co. Kildare
Ireland
www.merrionpress.ie

9781785373336 (Paper)
9781785373343 (Kindle)
9781785373350 (Epub)
9781785373367 (PDF)

British Library Cataloguing in Publication Data
An entry can be found on request

Library of Congress Cataloging in Publication Data
An entry can be found on request

Typeset in Bembo MT Std 11/15 pt

Front cover: John O'Neill, Bere Island, Co. Cork (back right) with
the Northumberland Fusiliers in Holland, September 1944.
Image courtesy of Sarah Bermingham.

Back cover: Major the Lord Rathdonnell receiving the Military Cross from
Field Marshal Montgomery, 12 August 1945. © Tyne & Wear Archives &
Museums/Bridgeman Images.

CONTENTS

The D-Day Landing

PHASE 1 **Airborne drop** Midnight–2AM *Over 13,000 paratroopers dropped behind enemy lines.*

PHASE 2 **Art of deceit** 1AM–4AM *The Allies faked another invasion in Pas de Calais.*

PHASE 3 **Aerial attack** 3AM *300 planes dropped 13,000 bombs on German defences.*

PHASE 4 **Naval attack** 5AM *Naval bombardment preceded the invasion.*

PHASE 5 **The invasion**

🔶 German batteries

🪂 Paratrooper drop zone

Areas captured by the Allies at midnight

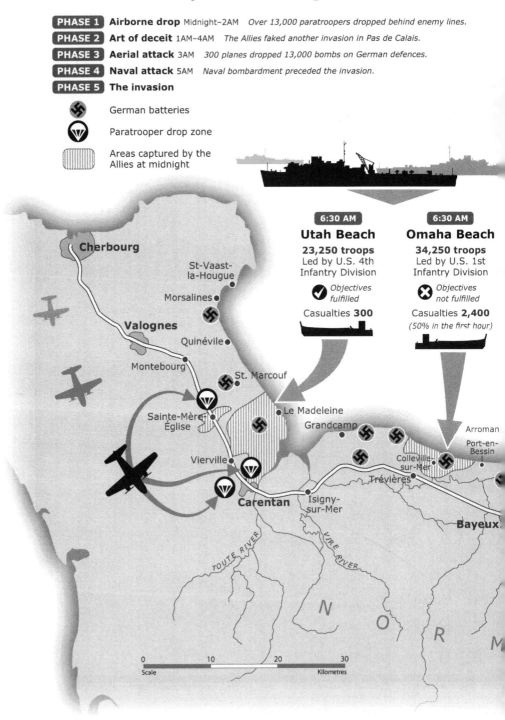

6:30 AM
Utah Beach
23,250 troops
Led by U.S. 4th
Infantry Division

✔ Objectives fulfilled

Casualties **300**

6:30 AM
Omaha Beach
34,250 troops
Led by U.S. 1st
Infantry Division

✖ Objectives not fulfilled

Casualties **2,400**
(50% in the first hour)

Cherbourg

St-Vaast-la-Hougue

Morsalines

Valognes

Quinéville

Montebourg

St. Marcouf

Sainte-Mère-Église

Le Madeleine

Grandcamp

Vierville

Carentan

Isigny-sur-Mer

Trévières

Colleville-sur-Mer

Arroman

Port-en-Bessin

Bayeux

TOUTE RIVER

VIRE RIVER

N O R M

0   10   20   30
Scale   Kilometres

6 June 1944

Supreme Commander
General Dwight D. Eisenhower

Soldiers: 156,000 troops
(73,000 U.S. Army, 83,000 British & Canadian)

Aircraft: 11,590

Navy: 6,939 vessels
(1,213 naval combat ships, 4,126 landing craft, 736 ancillary craft, 864 merchant vessels)
Navy personnel: 195,700 men
(52,889 U.S., 112,824 British, 4,988 other Allied countries)

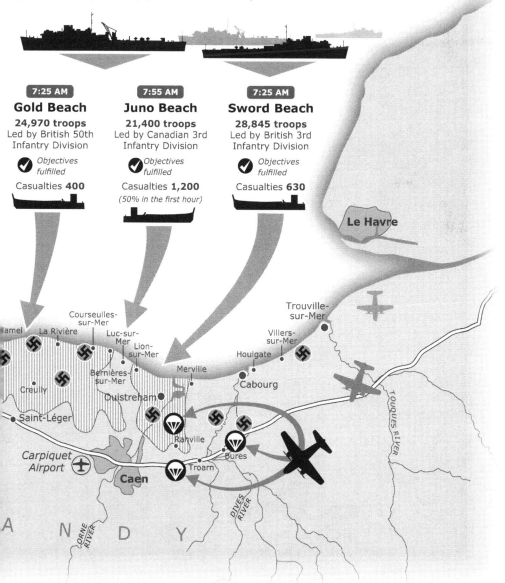

7:25 AM

Gold Beach
24,970 troops
Led by British 50th
Infantry Division

✔ *Objectives fulfilled*

Casualties **400**

7:55 AM

Juno Beach
21,400 troops
Led by Canadian 3rd
Infantry Division

✔ *Objectives fulfilled*

Casualties **1,200**
(50% in the first hour)

7:25 AM

Sword Beach
28,845 troops
Led by British 3rd
Infantry Division

✔ *Objectives fulfilled*

Casualties **630**

Le Havre

Trouville-sur-Mer

Courseulles-sur-Mer

Villers-sur-Mer

amel   La Rivière   Luc-sur-Mer   Lion-sur-Mer   Merville   Houlgate

Creuily   Bernières-sur-Mer   Cabourg

Ouistreham

Saint-Léger   Ranville

Carpiquet Airport ✈   Bures

Caen   Troarn

A   N   D   Y

ORNE RIVER   DIVES RIVER   TOUQUES RIVER

Operation
Market Garden

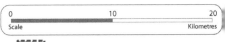
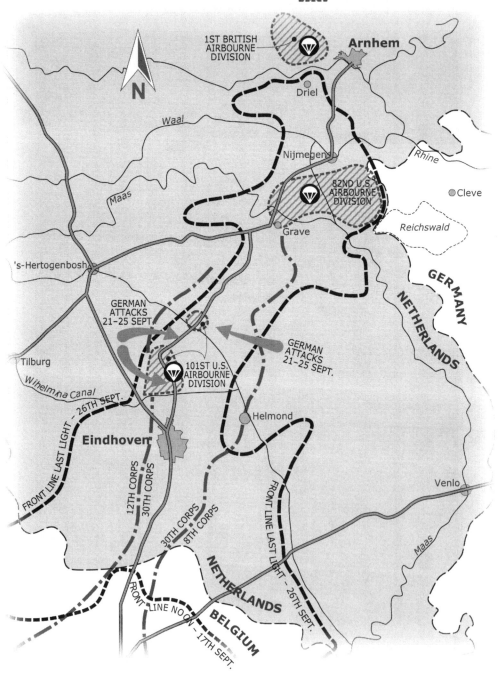

N

1ST BRITISH
AIRBOURNE
DIVISION

Arnhem

Driel

Waal

Nijmegen

Rhine

82ND U.S.
AIRBOURNE
DIVISION

Cleve

Maas

Reichswald

Grave

's-Hertogenbosh

GERMANY

NETHERLANDS

GERMAN
ATTACKS
21–25 SEPT.

GERMAN
ATTACKS
21–25 SEPT.

Tilburg

101ST U.S.
AIRBOURNE
DIVISION

Wilhelmina Canal

Helmond

FRONT LINE LAST LIGHT – 26TH SEPT.

Eindhoven

12TH CORPS

30TH CORPS

Venlo

30TH CORPS

8TH CORPS

FRONT LINE LAST LIGHT – 26TH SEPT.

Maas

NETHERLANDS

FRONT LINE NOON – 17TH SEPT.

BELGIUM

Ardennes German Offensive
(Battle of the Bulge)

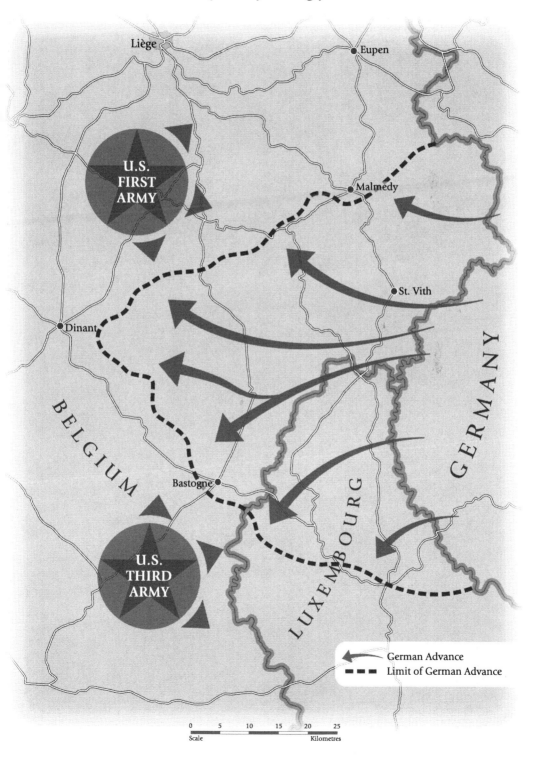

Liège

Eupen

U.S. FIRST ARMY

Malmedy

St. Vith

Dinant

GERMANY

BELGIUM

Bastogne

LUXEMBOURG

U.S. THIRD ARMY

German Advance

Limit of German Advance

0 5 10 15 20 25

Scale

Kilometres

Plunder Varsity Plan – Rhine River Crossing
(24 March 1945)

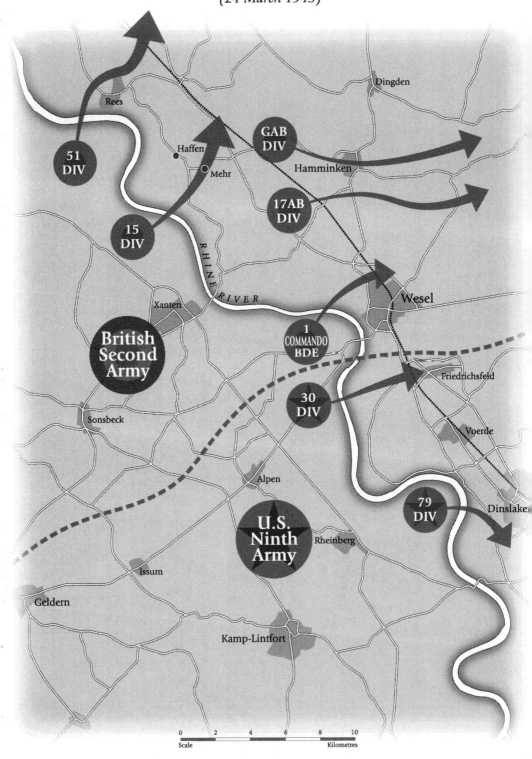

Dingden

Rees

GAB
DIV

Haffen

Mehr

Hamminken

51
DIV

17AB
DIV

15
DIV

RHINE

RIVER

Xanten

Wesel

British
Second
Army

1
COMMANDO
BDE

Friedrichsfeld

Sonsbeck

30
DIV

Voerde

Alpen

79
DIV

Dinslake

U.S.
Ninth
Army

Rheinberg

Issum

Geldern

Kamp-Lintfort

0   2   4   6   8   10
Scale   Kilometres

The Attack Towards and Encirclement of Berlin
(16–25 April 1945)

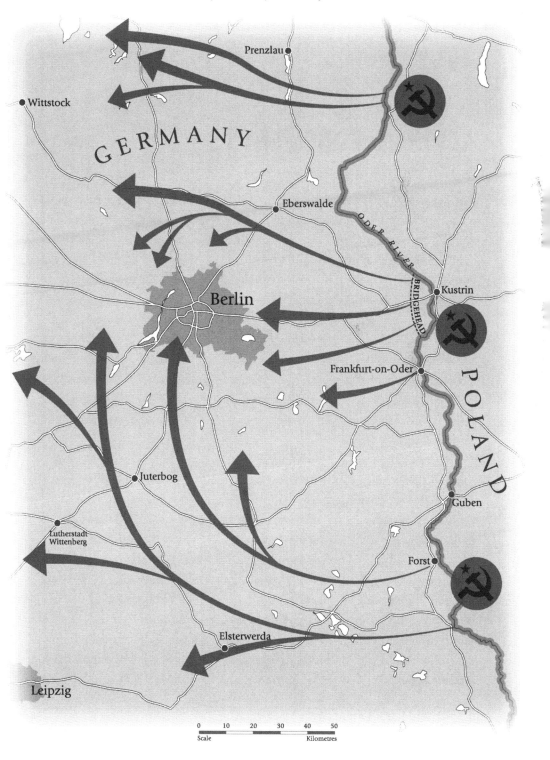

ACKNOWLEDGEMENTS

The Second World War was won with the help of the brave men and women who fought for the Allies in their hour of need. Those that took a principled stand against tyranny, for whatever motivation, ought to be respected rather than ignored. It is all too profound that it was an Irishman, Edmund Burke, who is attributed with the words, 'All that is necessary for the triumph of evil is that good men do nothing.'

When it mattered, the Irish did far from nothing. It is now an established fact that large numbers of Irish men and women fought with the Allies to save Europe from the evils of Nazi fascism. This is something that the Irish have become increasingly aware of over more recent decades. Because this involvement was more comprehensive than previously thought, it is now necessary to recalibrate our understanding of this heretofore underrated participation.

Ireland's double-edged ambiguity, arising from the State's pragmatic 'neutral' stance during the war, has created many misunderstandings and misperceptions, giving rise to much misinformation, whereas for many of the Irish there was a clear-cut course of action to be taken. The Irish were among the rangers, the commandos and the commanders; the airmen in the skies above and the sailors on the ships at sea. They all accepted the risks and exposed themselves to harm; they put themselves into the line of fire by entering deadly battle spaces, from the war's very beginning to its very end.

I wrote this book to make people aware that those Irish men and women who participated in the war were part of a broad, outward-looking nationalistic narrative, acting for Ireland and standing shoulder to shoulder with the Allies. On Remembrance Sunday 2019, at St Patrick's Cathedral in

Acknowledgements

Dublin, Canon David Oxley, the prebendary of St Audoen's, reported in *The Irish Times* that Irish neutrality in the Second World War was understandable from a political point of view. However, he added that, from a moral point of view,

> it was hardly possible to remain neutral in the face of the kind of evil represented by fascism. Many individual Irishmen and women did in fact take sides and volunteered to oppose Nazism in arms, and we commemorate their sacrifice this afternoon. And I suppose what I want to say to you is just this: in the conflict between right and wrong, truth and falsehood, neutrality is not an option.

These Irish men and women deserve our grateful appreciation and to be rightfully honoured – not written out of Irish history, taken off the beaches at D-Day, the bridge at Arnhem, the skies above in the Battle of Britain, or the many other battles during the war. Instead, they ought to be put centre stage; they ought to be in our school textbooks as examples of courage, character and commitment to steadfast values of resilience, fighting to maintain our freedoms, values and our democratic way of life. Indifference, indecision and uncertainty in the face of challenges to these freedoms are a threat – one which could unravel the very fabric and fortitude at the core of our being. Peace and freedom cannot be taken for granted and must be valued and defended.

I am grateful, therefore, to all those who gave me new information about those who contributed to the war effort. Specifically, I would like to thank Peter Byrne, Commandant (retd), who supplied an account of his cousin, US Ranger Sergeant Pearse Edmund 'Ed' Ryan, at Pointe du Hoc on D-Day. Thanks also to Tom Burns, who made me aware of his father James Gerald 'Jimmy' Burns and his participation with Bomber Command, and to Brian Wallace, who showed me the (flying) log book of his father, William Andrew 'Bill' Wallace, who was shot down over the beaches on D-Day. To Sarah Bermingham, who contributed detail about her uncle John O'Neill and his involvement at Arnhem, I am indebted. To Turtle Bunbury, who informed me of his grandfather William Robert McClintoch Bunbury, I am similarly thankful. Sincere thanks also to Conor Graham,

Acknowledgements

Maeve Convery and Patrick O'Donoghue at Merrion Press for handling the book's publication, Deirdre Maxwell for typing out the hand-written manuscript, Myles McCionnaith for editing the manuscript, and Paul O'Flynn for his technical assistance.

PREFACE

The Führer was dead. Hitler had ended his own life in his command bunker under the Reichstag Chancellery building in Berlin. German wireless transmitted an announcement on 1 May 1945 that Admiral Doenitz had been appointed to succeed him as Führer, and the Allies had picked up the news. Already long certain of the pointlessness of continuing hostilities, the Wehrmacht (German army) sent communications to the Allies to open negotiations for surrender. In response, the Allies had insisted on any terms being unconditional. A surrendering document was drawn up by the Supreme Headquarters Allied Expeditionary Force; the German delegation arrived in Reims to sign it, and when the German generals signed the unconditional surrender on 7 May, the Supreme Allied Commander in Europe, US General Dwight D. Eisenhower, asked Kay Summersby (formerly MacCarthy-Morrogh) from Inish Beg House, Baltimore, County Cork, to stand in the historic photographs and film. The war was over and at its official ending the Irish were there.

This was as appropriate as it was ironic, because at the very start of the war, on 4 September 1939, the day after hostilities began, 23-year-old pilot officer William Murphy, the son of William and Katherine Murphy of Mitchelstown, County Cork, was shot down and killed as he led a wave of Royal Air Force (RAF) bombers in an attack on the German naval port of Wilhelmshaven. All four bombers were lost. The sole survivor was Irishman Laurence Slattery of Thurles, County Tipperary. Willie Murphy's death was thus both the first Irish and British death of the Second World War and Laurence Slattery became the first and longest serving western Allied prisoner of war. From its very beginning to its end, and at all places, times and events in between, the Irish were there, fighting with the Allies, for freedom and democracy, against the terrible tyranny of Nazi fascism. This book is dedicated to those same selfless Irish men and women, both native-born and of Irish descent, whose involvement must be acknowledged and not forgotten; the values for which they fought and died must never be lost.

AUTHOR'S NOTE

Victory in Europe was declared. The war was over. The Germans had finally capitulated. In early May 1945, three different German delegations signed three separate surrender documents: for the British on 4 May in Lüneburg Heath; for the Americans on 7 May in Rheims; and for the Russians on 9 May in Berlin. Hitler had ended his own life at his command post in the Führerbunker near the Reich Chancellery building in Berlin. Within days, the heavily defeated German army surrendered, and the fighting had finally finished. Militarily overcome, the Nazi regime capitulated only because it was overwhelmingly overpowered and overrun. Germany had been made to yield.

Despite Allied and Russian victories at the Battle of Britain, Stalingrad and D-Day, each a turning point in the war, the fervour of the vehemently fanatical fascist regime had remained intact and so needed to be vanquished. It would have been entirely logical and proper for Germany to cease military operations; the Allies on the newly created Second Front had successfully achieved a lodgement, broken out at Normandy, liberated Paris, and driven fast eastwards, and the Russians on the Eastern Front were pressing westwards. It was irrational to believe that Germany could now succeed, but for the Third Reich it was intolerable to believe that they must now concede. An assassination attempt on Hitler having failed – Operation Valkyrie, on 20 July 1944 – the conflict continued. Instead of ending the war and suing for peace, the levels of hostility and horror increased. The resistance to the Allied advances across Europe intensified. There was no backward step; the Germans fought where they stood. Every city, town, river crossing and area of high ground on the Allied forces' advance was desperately defended. The

Germans, severely stricken, took heavy losses in personnel and territory, yet remained dangerously determined; every inch of the fatherland was bitterly contested.

With the Allies were the Irish – many Irish; thousands of Irish. At least 120,000 Irish in British uniform: 70,000 from the 'neutral' south, and 50,000 from the 'loyal' north. The story of the Second World War is enormous, and because the Irish populated its many events, they have a rightful place among its many chapters, something not readily acknowledged at home in Ireland, even today. This book, along with others in a series I have written on the Irish in the Second World War, attempts to excavate them from the corners of Irish history and place them back on the D-Day beaches, the bridge at Arnhem, the frozen landscapes at the Battle of the Bulge in the Ardennes, the banks of the Rhine River, into the unimaginable horrors of the Bergen-Belsen and Luckenwalde concentration camps, and at the Battle of Berlin itself. There was no one individual 'Irish Narrative', but there was a narrative of single individual Irish. Whichever way you look at it, the Irish were there. There was an Irish contribution, and it was a significant one. This book highlights the Irish involvement at the end of war, focusing on Irish participation from late 1944 until mid-1945. However, it does not presuppose knowledge on behalf of the reader, so included in the opening chapter of this book is a summarisation of the opening of the Second Front – the contribution of the Irish at D-Day and Arnhem. Both contributions were the subject of prior titles in the series; for those who have read these books, the summary here includes newly researched Irish involvement – that of native-born Irish and of the wider Irish diaspora – that have come to light since the prior books were published.

It is, I believe, important to be aware that the Irish were, in fact, there, and also to have an understanding of why. As ever, it was for a number of reasons: to seek adventure, for money, for family tradition. But it was also for altruistic reasons: many selflessly believed that Hitler had to be stopped, that he was a world problem, and that it was the best way to defend Ireland. Many of them agreed with the Irish State's neutral stance, but for them it was not enough; they had to do more and so became involved in actually fighting in the war. So who were they, and what did they do? I am privileged in granting them worthy mention.

I

THE SECOND FRONT

Confusion, mayhem and sheer terror greeted the US Rangers as the ramps of the first landing crafts hit the shore below the cliffs at the Pointe du Hoc promontory near Omaha Beach, situated in Normandy on the northern French coastline. Irishman Sergeant Pearse Edmund 'Ed' Ryan was born at 29 Cork Street, Dublin, in 1924; he and his parents immigrated to the USA the same year. The following is an account of his experience at dawn on D-Day, 6 June 1944, as recounted to the author by Ryan's cousin, Commandant Peter Byrne (retd):

> We were in the second wave, we had been delayed on the way from the troopship to the beach due to an adverse current or navigation or whatever. That delay might actually have saved some of us. As soon as we hit the water, the guy beside me had his head blown off. I mean it! It was surreal. There was no time to be shocked, sad or even to think! If you did so, you would surely panic. You just ignored the carnage around you and squeezing off the odd random shot from my M1 rifle I just prayed that I would not bring attention to myself, and with it the German machine gunners' aim. The automatic fire from above churned the sand around us. I am sorry to say that a small group of us dived to take cover behind the heaped bodies of some comrades from the first wave, who had fallen victim to the accurate MG-42 fire. I heard the sickening thud, thud, thud as bullets from the deadly Mauser [MG-42 machine gun] found their mark in the dead bodies again and again and again, but we were safe. Then there was a lull

when the German machine gunner needed to change ammo belts and we were away. A mad sprint to the bottom of the cliff and there, safe from view and from fire, we began to assess the utter havoc we were part of. Some guys threw up! This respite didn't last.

Galvanising the remaining assets at hand and assembling those of us still fit to fight, our officers ordered the ascent of the cliffs. We fired up rockets propelling ropes and grappling hooks but the soaking of the ropes in the seawater left them heavier than expected and some did not reach their target. 100 foot ladders were also deployed and soon I was heading up on one of those. I was told later that the long ladders had been supplied by the London Fire Brigade. With the crescendo of the MG-42s barking overhead, I full expected this to be my last day on earth and I whispered an abridged Act of Contrition to myself as I climbed the ladder. Just as I reached the top, another lull, silence as the machine gunner and his assistant changed belts to reload. Peeking over the top, I saw one of my comrades, already topside, approach the gun emplacement casemate with a satchel bomb. This is a small rucksack stuffed with RDX high explosive. He had ignited the pull switch fuse and the bomb was smokin'! I thought being killed thirty seconds later wouldn't make any difference so why don't I hang on to the ladder just below the cliff top and see how my buddy gets on! Kaaboom! He had lobbed that smoker right into the loophole [opening] of the casement, sending the MG-42 crew to kingdom come! Up and at 'em! The destruction of the main obstacle in our path injected a new energy into us Rangers as we piled up on the headland. I needn't tell you, we let rip. Myself and a buddy went around the back of a concrete bunker and found the steel door open. We had three grenades between us. I held the door and tossed in my grenade while he followed with his two. I slammed the door, hearing cries inside of 'Achtung, Achtung, Achtung!' which were answered by the grenades going Boom, Boom, Boom and the position was ours.

Pearse's unit suffered almost 50 per cent casualties in the action. They were gallantly led by a Texas farmer, Lieutenant Colonel James Earl Rudder, who was himself twice wounded in the action. 'Rudder's Rangers' quickly found and destroyed the 155mm Howitzers, but they had to hold out for two days against relentless German counterattacks, until they were finally reinforced on 8 June and the Germans withdrew. Holding out for those two days was a blur to Sergeant Ed Ryan; no sleep, no communications, no food, and perilously low on ammunition. But they had cracked the nut – they had taken the Pointe du Hoc clifftop battery: six 155mm Howitzer artillery guns in heavily reinforced concrete shelters; an impregnable position with formidable weaponry capable of flinging a 42kg high explosive shell nearly ten miles, with remarkable accuracy, from a commanding position dominating the landings at Utah and Omaha beaches. It was vital that these weapons would have to be captured or otherwise put beyond use. Having courageously fought their way to the clifftop, the rangers found, to their astonishment, that the gun emplacements were empty! Unknown, the Germans had withdrawn the artillery pieces during previous Allied aerial bombardments to avoid damage, hiding them nearby for rapid deployment, if required. Getting over their shock of finding telegraph pole dummies where the artillery pieces ought to have been, the real guns were looked for, found and destroyed. It had been one of the toughest missions handed down to any unit attacking Hitler's Atlantic Wall that D-Day dawn.

In an assault along a fifty-mile front, the Allies targeted five beaches codenamed Utah, Omaha, Gold, Juno and Sword on the Normandy coast. To defend against invasion, the Germans had built up a vast array of concrete coastal fortifications, artillery batteries, gun emplacements, minefields, barbed wire entanglements and improvised shoreline obstacles. In all, there were more than half a million men manning the shoreline obstacles from Holland's dykes to Brittany's peninsula, and even further north and south, from Norway to Spain. The Fifteenth Army, the Germans' main defensive force on the northern French coastline, was placed at the Pas-de-Calais, along the narrowest point of the English Channel between France and England. The Seventh Army, a less formidable one, was in Normandy. There was, however, a generally accepted belief that Calais, the shortest route and most direct to Berlin, with the most straightforward line of communications, was the most logical and therefore the most likely. It was also thought probable that the invasion would involve a support and a main attack, but which would be where?

Strictly speaking, Field Marshal von Rundstedt had territorial command but German Field Marshal Rommel had sought and been granted responsibility by Hitler to inject his energies, experience and enthusiasm into the situation. Rommel relished the challenge and his appointment to the post began with an inspection tour of the Atlantic Wall, only to find it far from being impregnable. A previous Allied coastal assault on Dieppe, in August 1942, had been defeated and proved costly for the Allies. The Germans had taken a certain amount of complacent comfort and even willing delusion from this. With Calais strongly suggesting itself as the foremost invasion site, it was here that Hitler had his Atlantic Wall heavily concentrated, its port strongly fortified and significant concrete coastal defences erected.

Elsewhere Rommel found many gaps, weaknesses and shortcomings along the defences of France's shoreline. He filled these identified weak points with further protections: pill boxes, gun emplacements (artillery set in reinforced concrete block house casements), mines and more mines. Rommel could not get enough mines. He was short of war materials, steel and concrete, and the labour force to build beach obstacles, so he adapted and improvised. He developed French conscript labour battalions, felled trees from woods and designed obstacles of his own, often with mines or fused shells placed on them. These crude, simple, unsophisticated-but-deadly barriers were erected in large numbers between high and low tide water marks. There were varying types, including concrete cones called 'dragons' teeth' and criss-crossing lengths of steel, some made from redundant railway tracks, which were cut and welded together in a jagged, protruding, triangular starfish shape. Another steel gate-like barrier configuration, known as 'Belgian Gates', and tree trunks, wooden beams and poles were set deep into the sand, projecting seawards, with mines or fused shells attached. All these were erected to repel the inshore invasion craft, to impale and rip open the hulls of landing craft, or cause damage or death with exploding mines and shells; they were to cause disruption and confusion, and to force disembarkation at the furthest point offshore, thus exposing the troops to gunfire for longer. Inland, Rommel had also flooded large areas of open field in order to counter parachutists or glider-borne troops likely to land there. Another defensive deterrent he used was to set poles in such spots, with barbed wire slung between the poles; this became known as 'Rommel's asparagus'. It was intended that these would tear apart the flimsy gliders as they attempted to land. Whatever preparations were possible, Rommel undertook them, driving his men hard and unapologetically. In doing so, he intended to conduct the defence of Europe at the water's edge, firmly convinced that the first twenty-four hours of the invasion would be vital.

D-Day was a bloody and terrifying battle; the horror of the events, the intensity of the fighting, the extent of the casualties and injured, were anticipated and planned for by the Allies. For months and even years ahead of the event, it was the fear of failure that occupied every waking moment of the D-Day invasion commanders, staff and planners. The consequences of failure were immense and the possibility of this was to haunt them incessantly and insidiously. The repercussions of a fiasco were huge, and there were no guarantees that it would not be a washout. If D-Day were not to succeed, if the planners had got it woefully wrong, not only would many deaths result on the day, but it would result in a lengthening of the war; the stark reality of extended fighting was many lives lost, a continuance of Nazi tyranny in Western Europe, and the potentially devastating effects of Hitler's V-1 and V-2 rockets, or flying bombs – 'the Doodlebugs', as the British public called them. There was also the extension of Hitler's secret weapons programme: the Messerschmitt Me 262, a jet-powered fighter prototype, and the V-3, a multi-barrelled gun capable of firing 140kg shells across the English Channel at a rate of one every six seconds – the so-called 'London Gun'. The turning point of the war (after the Battle of Britain in the summer of 1940) was the Battle of Stalingrad (August 1942–February 1943) with the Soviet victory over the Germans demonstrating that the soldiers of the supposed 'super race', the Wehrmacht, were not indestructible after all; following this, the advancing Red Army was threatening the frontiers of Germany, and perhaps beyond. Finally, there was the fear of the unthinkable: possible headway being made by German scientists developing an atom bomb for use!

It is fighting power that achieves objectives in the battlefield. To penetrate German defences demanded a build-up of military assets with force enough to overwhelm. If it were only that, it would be reasonably straightforward, militarily, but the plan also had to provide for an outmanoeuvring. The invasion troops had make it to shore and inland in sufficient numbers, with sufficient capabilities, to resist German counterattacks and maintain their forward thrust across Northwest Europe. The undertaking was breathtakingly enormous and the risks were immense, but it had to be done. The evil of Nazi fascism had to be halted, freedom preserved and democracy defended. A sense of the breadth of the onslaught is indicated in Lieutenant General Bernard Law Montgomery's D-Day briefing in St Paul's School, West London, on 15 May 1944:

> We must blast our way on shore and get a good lodgement before the enemy can bring sufficient reserves to turn us out. Armoured columns must penetrate deep inland, and quickly, on D-Day. This will upset the enemy plans and tend to hold him off while we build up strength. We must gain space rapidly and peg out claims well inland.

This invasion plan of Northwestern Europe had a geopolitical strategic context; it was advanced incrementally between the USA, Britain and Russia – that is, between Roosevelt, Churchill and Stalin – over a number of years. As a result, in March 1943, a combined Anglo-American military planning cell was established in London to oversee detailed proposals for the invasion plan. British Lieutenant General Frederick Morgan was appointed Chief of Staff to the Supreme Allied Commander (COSSAC) in order to begin planning for Operation Overlord. Getting ashore and forcing the invasion became the work of COSSAC planning staff. Surprise, strength, speed and sustainability were all important elements of this D-Day invasion plan. Selecting options of where to invade and keeping it secret while analysing associated issues posed a significant problem; seeking solutions to the issues kept the COSSAC planners busy throughout 1943.

Among their staff was Commander Rickard Charlie Donovan (Ballymore, Ferns, County Wexford), Royal Navy, who was part of the Plans Division – those co-ordinating Combined Operations (a branch of the Allied military HQ tasked with planning the invasion of Europe) – and so he became immersed in designing D-Day. An exceptional staff officer, he was retained after the war to write the history of Combined Operations. The strains of purism and pragmatism, combined together, also saw new technologies and tactics developed to tackle the beach obstacles; hard at work in this capacity was Irishman Michael Morris (later Lord Killanin), an officer in General

Percy Hobart's unique 79th Armoured Division – Hobart's parents were also both from Ireland. The 79th Armoured Division developed ingenious innovations, customising armoured vehicles to overcome Rommel's beach obstacles.

For their part, the Germans were also doing their planning. They knew the Allies were likely to use a support attack in co-ordination with – though not necessarily simultaneous to – the main assault. Perhaps the former as a feint, hoping to draw in the German reserves, and instead undertaking their main landing elsewhere. The Germans heavily analysed previous Allied amphibious landings in Morocco, Sicily and Salerno, and they believed they had a good grasp of how the Allies intended to fight their way ashore. However thorough, methodical and credible their examination and conclusions were, they were still left with the twin conundrums of where and when.

'Impracticable' had been the immediate verdict of General Montgomery, commander of the 21st Army Group (the land component commander for the invasion of Northwestern Europe). 'Monty' was from a family with deep roots in Moville, County Donegal, and was one of the best-known British generals of the Second World War; he oversaw victory over Rommel at the Battle of El Alamein, in North Africa (October–November 1942). When first shown the COSSAC D-Day plan very late in December 1943, Churchill immediately considered that the Allied assault needed to be widened from a twenty-five-mile front to a fifty-mile front, taking in five beaches instead of three, and that an additional air division be dropped prior to H-hour (the exact time when Allied invasion troops landed on the beach and the assault commenced). These suggested amendments, and others, were absorbed by the staff of the newly established Supreme Headquarters Allied Expeditionary Force (SHAEF) under General Eisenhower. The COSSAC plan had wisely prepared for what resources were actually available; the SHAEF plan prepared for what was actually needed, and Eisenhower had the authority to get whatever that might be, be it increased strength, ships or more time. His message to the troops on D-Day was as follows:

> You are about to embark upon the Great Crusade, toward which we have striven these many months.

The eyes of the world are upon you. The hopes and prayers of liberty-loving people everywhere march with you.

In company with our brave Allies and brothers-in-arms on other Fronts, you will bring about the destruction of the German war machine, the elimination of Nazi tyranny over the oppressed peoples of Europe and security for ourselves in a free world.

Your task will not be an easy one. Your enemy is well trained, well equipped, and battle-hardened. He will fight savagely.

On Monday 5 June 1944, 'Imminence of invasion is not recognisable' was the tone of Oberbefehlshaber West (OB West) in its estimate of Allied intentions, approved by Field Marshal von Rundstedt and sent to Oberkommando der Wehrmacht, the High Command of the Wehrmacht, later in the day. With the weather as it was and no apparent indicators to the contrary, they were comfortable in that assessment. In fact, many of the German high-level field commanders in OB West had been summoned to conduct a Kriegsspiel (tactical exercise without troops) away from the northern French coastline in order to prepare on maps at Rennes what was, ironically, about to unfold on the ground, on 6 June, at Normandy.

German Field Marshal Erwin Rommel (the Desert Fox) of Army Group B, after months of overseeing the defensive preparations against the Allies, intended to bring the Allied invasion to a grinding halt at the water's edge. Hitler, too, was convinced that the destruction of the Allied landings was the decisive factor in the entire conduct of the war, and would contribute significantly in its final result. Hitler had over-extended himself, fighting on two fronts at once. The decision to invade Russia in 1941, and his interference with his generals in the running of it, saw his offensive campaign on the Eastern Front culminating deep inside Russian territory – and the defeats began to mount. If the Germans could arrest the intended advance of the Allies in the west, Hitler could buy time and space, perhaps even discouraging the Allied army into reorganising and even reconsidering their options. If he succeeded in stopping them on the northern French shoreline, he could make a pact with Stalin or otherwise consolidate his still-not-inconsiderable military might on one front. As it was, most of the best of his forces were on the Eastern Front facing the Soviets. But the forces positioned on the

Western Front were not without strength, their resistance stiffened by the impregnable Atlantic Wall and the dogged leadership of Rommel.

While offence is the most decisive type of military operation, defence is stronger, and the Germans had prepared well. The invasion was due – even overdue. It had to come soon, but they did not know where or when. Wherever and whenever it did, they knew it would be a major turning point in the war. A spell of unseasonal and continuing bad weather, the worst seen in June along the northern French coastline in over twenty years, had convinced Rommel to feel confident that the Allied invasion was unlikely to occur over the coming days. And so, after months of devising and driving defence improvements, Rommel felt it appropriate to leave his headquarters in the castle of the Duke Francois de Rochefoucauld at La Roche-Guyon, roughly midway between Normandy and Paris, and make the eight-hour journey to his home in Herrlingen, Ulm, to celebrate his wife Lucie-Maria's birthday on 6 June. Rommel realised that the coming Allied attack would be decisive – in fact, that the first twenty-four hours of the invasion would be one of the most vital days of the war. What he did not realise was that the vast military machinery and apparatus of the greatest airborne and amphibious force ever assembled was already in motion and was about to unleash its massive might. The Longest Day, the Day of Days, was already at hand – the long-awaited Second Front was about to be opened.

The fate of the Second Front had become weather-dependent. Already Irish coastguardsman and Blacksod Lighthouse keeper Ted Sweeney, and his wife Maureen, had delivered a weather forecast by telephone from County Mayo's most westerly point. It was one of a number of weather stations feeding meteorological data updates on to Group Captain (Royal Air Force) J.M. Stagg's Meteorological Unit at Southwick House, southern England, to enable them to prepare and present advice to the Allied HQ on weather. The information update from Blacksod Lighthouse had given clarity to opinions of a previously divided prognosis among the US meteorologist staff – who were optimistic – and British staff – who were pessimistic – as to the effect of the prevailing adverse weather conditions: the successive depressions moving eastwards, twenty-four hours before the scheduled H-hour on 5 June. With first wave troops already aboard ships, General Eisenhower had suspended the operation; ships already out at sea had to be reversed and the fleet of ships that had not yet left harbour had to be kept quayside and the men left onboard. However, the second weather report from Blacksod suggested conditions likely to bring a brief interlude of improved weather. General Eisenhower, advised by Group Captain Stagg, launched D-Day with the famous words, 'OK, we'll go.'

And so started the largest airborne and seaborne invasion in history. Two hundred thousand Allied troops (Irish among them) hurled themselves headlong in a deadly onslaught against huge concrete German defence fortifications along Hitler's Atlantic Wall. It was an irresistible force against an immoveable object.

The Allied D-Day operation involved the execution of five interlinked and overlapping phases. Phase one: airborne paratrooper and glider-borne infantry drops – between midnight and 2 a.m. – with 23,000 troops descending behind the German lines, the US on the left or western flank and the British and Canadians on the right or eastern flank. Phase two: acts undertaken, between 1 a.m. and 4 a.m., to distract and deceive, even spreading the false perception that another point of attack was occurring at Pas-de-Calais. Phase three: aerial bombardment, at 3 a.m., with a heavy concentration on German coastal defences all along the northern French coast. Phase four: naval bombardment, at 5 a.m.; heavy salvos from Allied naval ships standing off the Normandy shoreline, covering the assault troop approach to shore on landing craft. Phase five: the first waves of Allied assault troops fight their way ashore, between 6 a.m. and 7.30 a.m., on five beaches, codenamed Utah, Omaha, Gold, Juno and Sword, over a fifty-mile stretch of enemy-held coastline; each was to breach the beach's defences, force their way inland to gain a lodgement in the hinterlands, and join up together in a consolidated bridgehead. Then they were to be prepared, once reinforced, to advance eastwards towards Paris.

The Germans along the Atlantic Wall were stationed in concrete constructions behind purpose-built structures of solid stone and steel. Where there were minefields and tank traps, Rommel had them enlarged and dug deeper; already-built bunkers were further reinforced. This was all done to channel the attacking Allied troops – and especially their tanks – to within range of carefully-sited anti-tank weapons and powerful Mauser MG-42 machine guns. These weapons, in addition to being placed in bunkers, were sited on the ground floors of fortified houses, beachfront villas, farmhouses inland and other 'strong point' buildings. These buildings, sturdy and ideal for adaptation, had been captured by the Germans and strengthened by buttressing them with logs, sandbagged earth and concrete. In some instances, entire coastal and inland villages were manipulated towards this end. These lines of beach and inland obstacles – minefields, bunkers, gun emplacements, fortified houses and resistance points – were a serious stumbling block for any attempted assault.

It was at the beaches, however, that the holding back of the Allied assault waves would occur – not indefinitely, necessarily, but for duration enough to allow the Panzer reserves to be brought forward and deployed, and then, with all their combined fire power, push the invasion back into the sea. Rommel wanted these Panzer divisions already present at the coast, primed and prepared, during the first hours of the invasion, to drive the Allies back into the sea in what he foresaw as a violent and brutal defence. The Panzers were not available to him, however; instead they were held far back and only to be released on Hitler's direct orders. Rommel doubted that they would not arrive on time; in fact, he believed they would not arrive at all. They would become stalled, or more likely completely destroyed, by Allied aircraft, as the Allies had almost unfettered air superiority.

Availing of this air superiority was Dubliner William 'Bill' Andrew Wallace; he flew a Seafire aircraft, a naval version of the Spitfire which was adapted for operation from aircraft carriers. A pilot with the Royal Navy Volunteer Reserve, he was part of Fleet Air Arm's 867 Air Squadron. His D-Day log book entry records that he was spotting for HMS *Warspite*, calling in the fall of shot of their gun salvos to increase their accuracy. It also notes that he was shot down over a beachhead at 8.30 a.m. and landed near Russy crossroads, five miles inland, behind enemy lines! Flak from anti-aircraft guns had hit his engine and he force-landed in fields, his engine on fire. With assistance from locals, who gave him directions as to where the Germans were, he managed to avoid being captured and navigated his way to the American beachhead 'O', spending the night on the English Channel on board an American landing craft tank. Bill, the son of the porter of the Northern Bank on Dublin's Grafton Street, who grew up in a flat above the bank, arrived safely back to England and survived the war; he later joined

Aer Lingus, where he worked for twenty-four years, and in 1970 he became one of the first pilots to join Aer Arann. Bill died in 1985.

Another pilot who came to earth, this time on purpose, was Irish-born Oliver Plunkett Boland, a glider pilot. He was the second glider to land at Pegasus Bridge in undoubtedly one of the most daring and well-executed actions by the British 6th Airborne Division; it was a pre- H-hour 'coup-de-main' operation to seize and hold two bridges, keeping them intact for later use by the Allies. Crash-landing their gliders, with expert precision, immediately adjacent to the bridge, the men from 2nd Oxfordshire and Buckinghamshire Light Infantry (the Ox and Bucks) and 249 Field Company Royal Engineers, all commanded by Major John Howard, surprised a stunned bridge guard, overwhelming them with staggering speed, grenades and small arms fire; it was no small feat. Well after the war, in conversation with Irish journalist Kevin Myers, who asked him if there were Irish men among the Ox and Bucks regiment, now-retired Major John Howard replied, 'about ten per cent', then adding, 'the best ten per cent!' Those under Major Howard were later reinforced by the 7th Parachute Regiment; together they successfully held the bridges until further reinforced on D-Day by Lord Lovat's 1st Special Service (Commando) Brigade, who landed on Sword Beach.

Among the ranks of the reinforcements was Galwegian Private Pat Gillen, who described his exit from his landing craft in the following terms, 'The whole thing was to move fast, not to be an object for the snipers. They used to say "if you want to see your grandchildren then get off the landing craft faster than Jessie Owens [an Olympic sprinter]". Seemingly I was fast.'

Thousands upon thousands of Allied assault troops ran that gauntlet and diced with death, disembarking, under intense enemy fire, onto the D-Day beaches, at dawn on 6 June 1944. Many died, but the carnage was especially horrible in the opening hours on Omaha Beach. Among the first to die on Omaha was Joseph Madagan, whose mother was from Clouna, near Ennistymon in County Clare. Joseph was with the US Rangers, who, alongside 'A' Company 116th Infantry Regiment, were among the first wave. Weighed down with heavy backpacks and equipment, staggering and stumbling through water, those moving sluggishly were easily picked out by the enemy snipers. Earlier, Allied aerial and naval bombardments, although immense, had not always achieved the desired results, and there was plenty of fight left in the defenders.

But it was the Allies, with naval support, tank fire, air support and the sheer grit of courageous small units, that won the day; by day's end, the Allies had a foothold on the Normandy coast. Most survived the horrors of D-Day, but many fell in the fierce fighting in *bocage* countryside: the small fields, high hedgerows, earthen embankments and sunken roads which were ideal for the wily and determined German defenders, who still had considerable resolve left.

The Germans had been surprised by the Allied landing at Normandy, and, significantly, continued to believe, as they had been led to believe, that the Allied invasion at Normandy was only a diversion for a still-to-be-executed main Allied effort at the Pas-de-Calais. They had become convinced by their own logic – with assistance from the Allies – of a phantom army that was poised to strike across the English Channel from Dover. This highly successful Allied deception continued to keep the Germans' very real and very strong Fifteenth Army in situ to fight a very fake First United States Army Group formation.

The Allied penetration inland was not going as fast as hoped for, and certain key cities – Bayeux, Caen, Carentan and Saint-Lô – took a lot of fighting to capture. The Allies had done well, but they experienced a lot of intense and bloody fighting in the *bocage*. After three weeks of this, US Ranger Sergeant Ed Ryan, who had successfully scaled the cliffs and captured the gun emplacements at Pointe du Hoc, was shot and wounded. He survived the war. Also wounded was Lance Corporal James Bryan, a farm labourer from Thurles; he fought with 3rd Battalion Irish Guards on D-Day, sustaining the injury on 9 July, outside Caen, from a German Stuka dive bomber. Shot in the neck by a sniper was Dubliner John Donnelly, whose obituary in *The Irish Times*, 15 June 2019, tells us that, apart from fighting with the British army, landing on Sword Beach on D-Day, he became one of Ireland's foremost insolvency experts after the war and lived to be ninety years of age. John Donnelly lost many friends as a young soldier, and this affected him very deeply. It was perhaps this fact that led him to spend two years training for ordination as a Jesuit, and, later, to have a short-lived dalliance as a medical student. In time he settled down in his father's chartered accountancy practice, which he bought out two years before qualifying himself.

James 'Jim' Sullivan was conscripted at Reading, England. He was a point-to-point jockey at Wantage in the United Kingdom. A member of 51st Highland Division, he was part of the British Expeditionary Force (BEF) evacuated from Dunkirk, on 4 June 1940, on a ship called *The Princess Maud* along with 1,270 others. Later, as a tank driver attached to the 7th Armour Division ('The Desert Rats'), he took part in the North African campaign; on the way back from this campaign he became involved in the invasion of Sicily, then returning to the UK to prepare for D-Day. Wounded on the approach to Caen, he was brought back to the Royal Memorial Hospital at Netley, Southampton, and on recovery he was sent back to Salisbury. His younger brother Denis also served in the British army during the war, with the 16th Carrier Platoon, while his three other brothers, Donal, Jerry and William 'Bill' Sullivan served in the Irish Defence Forces.

The hard fighting on the ground involved three separate operations to try to take Caen. Heavy aerial bombardments of German defences became a feature of the bloody struggle, with casualties mounting on both sides. Progress through the *bocage* was painfully slow and cost the lives of many men and a lot of materials. That it was not unnecessarily slow was always a concern of General Montgomery, who was criticised by his detractors for being overly cautious but praised by the soldiers for not being wantonly wasteful with their lives – a lesson Monty had learned personally on the Western Front during the First World War.

Fixing the Germans into positions and wearing away their strength, the various Allied (British and Canadian) operations were actually achieving what they were designed to. The outcome was in line with the operational narrative Montgomery had envisaged; the uncertainty and delayed timelines frustrated many, however. Meanwhile, the hard fighting and dying continued on the ground. Allied aerial and artillery bombardments had a brutal physical effect on the Germans, and where this was not actually the case, the psychological impact caused many to become dazed, even demoralised and some practically 'demented'. Drawing in the Germans on the east flank of the bridgehead, keeping them there, and making them commit their reserves of men and, more particularly, their tanks, allowed the Americans on the west flank to push southwards, facing minimum resistance; next they turned eastwards, then sweeping northwards and creating a pincer movement with the British and Canadians. This manoeuvre forced open the 'breakout' as the Allies finally penetrated the Germans' fiercely defensive posture. This was Monty's battle plan, and even though it took longer than first assessed, the strategy eventually worked. The fighting in the *bocage* was behind them. The Germans fell back in disarray and narrowly avoided annihilation at the Falaise Pocket, where the encircling Allies failed to close the gap quickly enough. There was much left to do and a second, much smaller, amphibious invasion of France in the southeast, near Nice and Marseilles – known as Operation Dragoon – which was successfully completed on 15 August. The liberation of Paris quickly followed and the Allies swept eastwards, at speed, making a rapid advance towards Germany. Their momentum was curbed on the Dutch border due to highly extended supply lines that still stretched all the way back to Normandy. The port of Antwerp was in Allied hands; the difficulty was that it was forty miles inland and the Germans still had control of the Scheldt estuary, which led from the sea to Antwerp.

With the Allied advance stalled due to a shortage of supplies – particularly of fuel and ammunition. The Red Ball Express, the convoy system which was its lifeline, could not keep up the flow of supplies needed to maintain an advance against the German resistance. In order to continue to capitalise on the Germans' confusion, the Allies needed to be hot on the heels of their retreat. The Germans were not to be given time and space to reorganise and recover. Along the Belgium–Netherlands border, considerations of time and space, Monty felt, were best addressed by surprise and speed; airborne surprise combined with the speed of XXX Corps (30 Corps) were the keys to success.

It was not, however, the newly-promoted Field Marshal Montgomery's decision to make, because on 1 September 1944 General Dwight D. Eisenhower assumed direct operational command and control of all Allied ground forces in Europe. Monty was no longer the overall co-ordinator of the land battle – an appointment he had been granted by Eisenhower for the D-Day assault and the Battle of Normandy. This, of course, had placed American troops under Montgomery's command; back in the US, public opinion turned against this, due to the already superior number of American troops in Europe and the ever-increasing US contribution, of equipment and supplies, to the Allied cause.

It had been Eisenhower's intention to drive forward on a broad front, forcing the now-unsettled Wehrmacht to try and cope with many points of Allied attack simultaneously. However, the slowly arriving supplies meant he was unable to exploit US General Patton's advance in the south and Montgomery's in the north. Both had an intense dislike of the other and they had a longstanding rivalry – each wanted to beat the other to Berlin.

Montgomery wanted the Germans kept on the run; he felt the pressure needed to be kept on them, so in the absence of a plan from Eisenhower's headquarters, he devised one of his own which would provide 'a really powerful and full blooded thrust'. Montgomery's audacious plan was untypical of his usual slow, considered, meticulously-built-up approach; it was bold, risky, even reckless.

With the success of D-Day, the Battle of Normandy, and the collapse of German resistance in France and Belgium, the end of the war was within sight. Monty's Operation Market Garden was undertaken to further this end. Imaginative, daring, simple – the 'Market' part of the operation was the surprise element, involving US and British paratroopers who were to seize some seven main bridges, laying a carpet, as it were, for the 'Garden', or speed element, of the British XXX Corps, who were to advance rapidly up this 'corridor' – a single sixty-four-mile access road to Arnhem. This was to be the start line for a further operation, avoiding the defences of the Siegfried Line (the Western Wall), instead heading into the Ruhr, the German industrial heartland. This, it was hoped, would end the war before Christmas 1944, saving tens or even hundreds of thousands of lives. The US 82nd and 101st airborne divisions seized and held their objectives, although it was not in total keeping with the planned timeline. The most difficult task, the seizing and holding of the bridge farthest away at Arnhem, fell to the British 1st Airborne Division and 1st Polish Parachute Brigade. There were Irishmen throughout the Operation Market Garden formations, and not least at Arnhem, where hundreds were involved in the fierce fighting.

D-Day was planned over months, even years. The planning for Operation Market Garden took place over days, scarcely a full week. It was the first time the Allies used airborne troops strategically. Nothing like it, in terms of scale, had ever been attempted before. Thirty-five thousand airborne troops were flown a distance of three hundred miles from England. It was the first time the First Allied Airborne Army was to be deployed after nine previous cancelled operations; they were itching to get into the fight before the war was over. There had been an over-optimism and over-simplification of the situation, and a belief by some – Lieutenant General Frederick Montague 'Boy' Browning chief among them – that all the airborne army had to do was get airborne and victory would follow. Then came the realisation that there were simply not enough aircraft to drop three-and-a-half airborne divisions in one day. Thereafter, Lieutenant General Lewis Hyde Brereton's air plan shaped how the airborne insertion would happen. In the event, the plan was overly weighted toward the consideration of loss of aircraft; the drop zones selected were too far away from the objectives and the Allies lost the essential element of surprise, tying up manpower having to protect the landing and drop zones instead of fighting for the bridge. It was a day drop and there was no fighter or fighter bomber support – a stipulation by Major General Paul L. Williams, IX Troop Carrier Command that handed air superiority to the Germans. The asset of fire power was lost, as was the Allied ability to help break deadlock situations, protect troops and press home advantages. Bad luck, poor weather and ineffective radio communications all played their part, but another significant factor in the unsuccessful seizure of Arnhem bridge was regarding intelligence – the known presence of two German Panzer divisions in the vicinity was ignored. Dutch underground reports, photo reconnaissance and Ultra code interceptions all gave strong indications of their existence. Any delays, however, did not suit the many prevailing agendas at play. Chief among them was that Allied Command wanted to test the capability of the First Allied Airborne Army's capacity; its commanders wanted to get into the war before it was over and be able to point towards their operational experience. Churchill wanted the German V-1 and V-2 rocket launching sites overrun while Montgomery wanted to regain control of Allied strategy; Eisenhower wanted an end to the squabbling between Patton and Montgomery, and maybe to get a Rhine crossing into the bargain. Overall, there was a sense that Germany had little left to offer by way of halting the Allied advance; they were on the ropes and one knockout blow was all that was needed to bring the war to a close; 1944 was 1918 all over again, and the dramatic collapse of German resistance was once again at hand. Caution was not a part of the prevailing mindset, and, given the top-down endorsement of the Market Garden plan, neither was it felt that the suggestion of such circumspection would have been appreciated.

On 17 September 1944, Lieutenant Colonel 'Joe' Vandeleur, Irish Guards, gave the order to his lead tank commander to cross the 'start line' and set in motion XXX Corps' advance up the route that became known as 'Hell's Highway' – the 'Garden' part of Operation Market Garden commenced. Progress up Hell's Highway was marred by delay, ambushes and blown-up bridges; the rate of advance fell well behind schedule. So much so that, in Arnhem, those who were tasked with holding the bridge for two days were still there eight days later, fighting in vain, not only to establish an alternative bridgehead at the Oosterbeek perimeter, but also for their very lives. This fight against a rapidly reinforced German opposition saw the 1st Airborne Division suffer enormous casualties (fatalities and wounded), and prisoners of war were taken. Only a dramatic, organised withdrawal back across the Lower Rhine, under the cover of darkness and artillery covering fire, saved what remained of the shattered airborne division. Thwarted in their efforts to secure the last bridge – the major objective of the operation – the Allies now had to reconcile themselves to the fact that the war would extend beyond Christmas, likely well into 1945.

John O'Neill, from Bere Island off Castletownberehaven in County Cork, was one among those who had lost their lives. He had followed two brothers to Worcestershire in 1933 and three years later enlisted in the British army. He fought with the Northumberland Fusiliers and was killed in action; he was 29 years of age, and is buried in Overloon War Cemetery in the Netherlands.

Sergeant John Daly from County Waterford, 1st Airlanding Light Regiment, was one who received reward for his efforts; he was awarded the Distinguished Conduct Medal for providing covering fire with a Bren light machine gun, allowing Major Robert Cain, South Staffordshire Regiment, to successfully stalk and ambush Tiger tanks – for which Cain was awarded the Victoria Cross (VC). Cork man John Stout served with the Irish Guards Armoured Division, which raced to Arnhem and came agonisingly close to capturing the key bridge.

Brigadier General John 'Shan' Hackett, Officer Commanding 4th Parachute Brigade, was one of the very last back across the Lower Rhine, well after the organised withdrawal; he was the son of a Tipperary man and Trinity College graduate who had immigrated to Australia. He had hidden out, with the help of local Dutch residents, for weeks after the battle. The Germans had imposed restrictions on the distribution of food against these same local residents, along with others in the urban areas of the western part of the Netherlands, leading to severe shortages in what became known as the 'Hungerwinter', during which people starved and died. Their already perilous plight was added to by a bitterly cold winter, the freezing conditions exacerbating their suffering. A plan – Operation Manna – was devised by the British to airdrop food supplies to the needy population. Belfast-born Air Commodore James Roy 'Paddy' Forsyth was one of the pilots who took part in this RAF humanitarian mercy mission, which succeeded in dropping some 6,500 tonnes of supplies.

Lieutenant Colonel John Place from Foxrock, Dublin, Commanding Officer No. 2 Wing RAF Glider Pilot Regiment, was the pilot of a Horsa glider during Market Garden; while map-reading, he suddenly had to take over the controls when a piece of shrapnel from an exploding shell outside the cockpit window pierced the fuselage of the glider and fatally wounded co-pilot Ralph Alexander Maltby, from Belfast, who was flying the glider at the time. As they neared the landing zone, machine-gun fire ripped through the plywood fuselage, wounding another of the occupants. Nevertheless, Lieutenant Colonel Place managed to bring the glider down in a safe and successful landing.

Another Dublin connection involved the actress Audrey Hepburn, whose mother was a Dutch noblewoman. Both her parents were sympathetic towards the British Union of Fascists in the mid-1930s, and her father suddenly left the family to become more deeply involved in their activities. Hepburn and her mother went to Kent, where she was educated, before moving to her mother's farm in Arnhem. Her parents divorced in 1938. It is believed that while there Hepburn raised money for the Dutch resistance through her performances in silent ballet dance and witnessed the transportation by train of Dutch Jews to concentration camps. Hepburn, too, suffered during the subsequent German blockade of food supplies, and she became ill. However, success and fame awaited her as a Hollywood actress, during which time, in 1960, she renewed contact with her father after locating him in Dublin through the Red Cross. While he remained distant, emotionally, she financially supported him for the rest of his days.

The Allies were poised on the German frontier, their advance hampered by a shortage of supplies. Montgomery's bold gamble to 'jump the Rhine' at Arnhem had not worked and Allied forces again focused on securing the Scheldt estuary – approaches to which were held by the Germans – in order to free up the use of Antwerp Port, which was in their own hands. The failure to secure Arnhem was a setback; Montgomery's surprise drive towards Berlin was a failed gamble at bringing an end to the Second World War. Now it was time for an emboldened Hitler to launch his own.

2
THE BATTLE OF THE BULGE

Following confusion and collapse, the German defensive line had hastily regrouped. Despite consternation over a continually dwindling front line, the Germans had demonstrated toughness and a dynamic ability to manage adversity and operate under extreme pressure. They had halted the Allied headlong advance towards Germany. The Allied forces' inability to maintain a viable logistical pipeline and supply the battle area meant a shortage eventually manifested itself, holding back the Allied attacking momentum. Also, the failure to close the Falaise Gap ('the German Dunkirk') and the all-too-slow pursuit of the retreating Pas-de-Calais-based German 15th Army by the Canadians meant substantial numbers of Germans escaped capture.

Massive and menacing; bold, intimidating and ruthless; organised and dangerous, Hitler's war machine was a formidable force, greatly feared and brutally effective. The fascist Nazi regime sought world domination over all peoples by the one 'super race'. The Normandy landings on 6 June 1944 made history; it was a day when the courage of men (Irish men and women among them) tackled the Germans' terrible tyranny. At stake was the future shape of Europe; it was a turning point in history. As it happened, the challenge of opening the Second Front proved successful.

The earlier, and first, defeat of the Germans by the Russians at Stalingrad (August 1942–February 1943) on the Eastern Front was a merciless, gruesome and vicious struggle, a human hell of a battle, with fierce hand-to-hand, man-to-man fighting inside an urban area; there was a lot of brutal close-quarter carnage. It proved hugely destructive to the German army, whose failed invasion of Russia – Operation Barbarossa – saw Hitler's expansionist ambitions forced into decline. The subsequent Allied landings at Sicily and Salerno in Italy put further pressure on the Axis powers, despite frequent stalemate. The sheer scope of the Normandy landings on D-Day, the gathering of such military might, was unimagined by the Germans; once the Allied 'breakout' from Normandy was achieved, it saw the Germans back peddling at pace – they were hastily retreating and fighting on all fronts. Blitzkrieg ('Lightning War') offence had given way to a desperate defence, its toll on human life enormous.

And yet the fanaticism of Nazi party chiefs meant that the war went on; the killings kept happening and SS brutality continued. Despite Allied and Russian armies pressing hard on both frontiers, the Germans squeezed relentlessly in the middle, the collapse of the Wehrmacht imminent, the war virtually lost and revenge by the Red Army savage, Hitler still would not yield.

'Wonder weapons' were part of Hitler's planned response. Already the world had seen him deploy these Vergeltungswaffe ('retaliatory weapons') with the V-1 flying bombs. Unmanned aircraft loaded with explosives had been directed towards London and other British cities, their flight time calculated – their purpose to destroy civilian targets and to demoralise. These 'buzz bombs' or 'Doodlebugs', as the British public called them, had first arrived in London on 10 June 1944. Ten were fired that day and six hit London; thereafter, from launch sites along the English Channel, one hundred of them arrived each day. It is estimated that up to 10,000 V-1s fell on England before the launch sites were overrun by Allied ground troops, but not before they had caused some 20,000 casualties (deaths and injuries). On 8 September, the second of the 'miracle weapons' from his secret weapons programme was launched, the V-2. It was a larger, more sophisticated and deadly rocket, fired from mobile launch pads. In all, about a thousand landed in British cities, with little or no effective response. They were only stopped when Allied ground troops took and and held ground, pushing them back out of range.

Of crucial importance was the taking and holding of the Scheldt estuary; taking control of it would bring the deep water inland port of Antwerp into use. Its denial as a component in the Allied logistical pipeline was now the main factor holding back future advance. The Allied advance was in danger of grinding to a halt and Monty's daring but reckless plan, Operation Market Garden, a concentrated, sudden attack on a broad front, had failed. A standstill resulted, so within a fortnight the Allies launched another attack to break the deadlock. The First Canadian Army, with Polish and British units attached, was tasked with clearing the Scheldt estuary of the German 15th Army, which held the mouth of the River Scheldt and deprived the Allies of the crucial Antwerp port. In addition, the Germans had fortified the strategically important Walcheren island with massive coastal artillery guns, which were well protected from aerial bombardment. German General Gustav-Adolf von Zangen, Commander of the 16th Army, reportedly told the defenders:

> after overrunning the Scheldt fortifications, the English would finally be in a position to land great masses of material in a large and completely protected [90 per cent intact] harbour. With this material they might deliver a death blow at the North German plain and at Berlin before the onset of winter … The enemy knows that he must assault the European fortress as speedily as possible before its inner lines of resistance are fully built up and occupied by new divisions. For this, he needs the Antwerp Harbour. And for this reason, we must hold the Scheldt fortifications to the end. The German people are watching us. In this hour, the fortifications along the Scheldt occupy a role which is decisive for the future of our people. Each additional day will be vital that you deny the port of Antwerp to the enemy and the resources he has at his disposal.

The Allied push to clear the way along the Scheldt estuary – the Battle of the Scheldt (2 October–8 November 1944) – and remove the German threat proved slow-going. It involved three weeks of tough amphibious assaults, obstacle-crossing and costly fighting over open ground in order to clear the route along the estuary to the river's mouth. It took a further week to overwhelm the Germans and take the Walcheren island. In all, there were 13,000 Allied casualties. Royal Navy minesweepers then went to work and cleared the numerous sea mines in the river. On 28 November, the first supply ships reached Antwerp; the Allies could now move forward again.

Captain Redmond Cunningham, 1st Troop Leader, 5 Assault Regiment, 79th Assault Squadron of the Royal Engineers, from Waterford, had already won the Military Cross for his beach-clearing actions on Sword Beach on D-Day. His troop of Armoured Vehicle Royal Engineers (AVRE) consisted of a Crab tank, with its two mine-clearing flails, a Bridge tank, a fascine, with its bundle of logs designed to fill in anti-armour ditches and, finally, a Bobbin, which used a metal carpet to make the path across soft-going terrain (mud or sand) traversable. The other varieties of modified tanks, custom-designed for obstacle crossing, were the Crocodiles – flame-throwing tanks with a range of 150 yards – the Petard tanks, with their bunker-busting spigot mortar guns, and the Firefly tanks – Sherman tanks fitted with the British 17-pounder anti-tank gun. Later on during D-Day, inland, he had been ordered to take ten AVREs with which to seize and hold the bridge and lock gates at Ouistreham. Using the not-inconsiderable firepower of the ten AVREs, the bridge and lock gates were wrestled from the Germans. These were successfully held overnight – a duration which saw active patrolling under Captain Cunningham's direction and resulted in the capture of enemy positions, materials and prisoners. During the Battle of the Scheldt four months later, his offensive-mindedness again saw him awarded a decoration – a bar to his Military Cross – when he led an assault on German positions, capturing some 200 prisoners. It was there that Cunningham was to receive the shrapnel wounds that he would carry with him for the rest of his life. He was awarded a Croix de Guerre by the Belgian government for his part in rescuing civilians in Antwerp following a German V-1 attack on the centre of the city. Hitler, furious that it was once again operational, ordered his V-weapons deployed. At war's end, Redmond Cunningham qualified as an architect and became involved in many successful business ventures in Waterford. He died in 1999. With the estuary and Antwerp port in Allied hands, and again fully operational, dredged deep enough to allow the passage and docking of ocean-going ships, the Allies could again move forward. Only then, the weather changed. Autumn rains poured down, turning the battlefields into quagmires. The Allied advance had to halt once more, waiting for spring to renew the advance. Meanwhile, the Germans, in their weakened state, were thought to be preserving their resources for the impending Russian assault on their Eastern border. Only they weren't.

Taking the Allied totally by surprise, Hitler launched a sudden attack on the Western Front. He hit the Allied line at its flimsiest point – in the forested, hilly Ardennes area in Belgium – with the might of 200,000 troops and 1,000 tanks and tank destroyers. He had successfully assembled his last remaining strategic reserve of troops in total secrecy. Despite being hugely outnumbered, desperately short of fuel, and lacking air support, the German army had successfully concealed the build-up of this strike force – Allied intelligence had missed it completely. The plan was to burst through the Ardennes hills with one powerful punch, swing north, split the British and American armies, retake Antwerp port, cutting the Allied Supply Line once again. Operation Herbstnebel ('Operation Autumn Mist'), also known as *Wacht am Rhein* ('Watch on the Rhine'), caught the disbelieving Allies completely off guard, beginning at 6 a.m. on 16 December 1944 when German artillery opened up in advance of tanks and infantry, driving successfully through an eighty-five-mile stretch of the lightly defended sector of the Allied front line. Further incredulity arose from German commandos, proficient in English, dressed in American uniforms, and driving US jeeps – captured in Arnhem – and disguised tanks, successfully infiltrating Allied lines to carry out chaos and commit acts of sabotage. The impact of this subterfuge was largely psychological. Its effect on US troops was to engender a certain degree of paranoia and mistrust; road block positions were established and a set of authentication questions were asked that only 'true' Americans would likely know the answers to. In such an atmosphere, rumour and unconfirmed hearsay spread – some even believing the story that the German commandos' real intent was to kill General Eisenhower. Concern about this possible threat was taken seriously and saw Eisenhower temporarily confined to his Versailles headquarters. This German commando-type special forces unit was mostly composed of foreign recruits whose commanding officer was an Austrian, Lieutenant Colonel Otto Skorzeny. The unit had been successful in a glider-borne rescue of Hitler's ally, Benito Mussolini, from the highly defended Italian mountaintop hotel where he was incarcerated after having been overthrown.

Intriguingly, there were two Irish men who, through a series of unfortunate events, found themselves, at one stage, among the commandos' ranks. Terence O'Reilly, in *Hitler's Irishmen*, tells us that James Brady and

Frank Stinger, in 1938, had joined the Royal Irish Fusiliers, and were posted to Guernsey in the English Channel in 1940. One evening in Guernsey, drunk, they were denied service in a local pub. They became disorderly, were arrested, and were incarcerated in police cells. When the island was occupied by the Germans, the Guernsey police handed the men over to them. Initially, as prisoners of war of the Wehrmacht, they were taken to Camp Friesack in Brandenburg, Germany, and put to work as farm labourers, thereafter taking up an offer to become members of a German military unit – the unit turned out to be that of Lieutenant Colonel Otto Skorzeny.

If Brady and Stinger had been part of the alleged attempt to assassinate Eisenhower, it would have brought them into contact with those around him – one of whom was fellow Irish countrywoman, Kay Summersby (Kathleen McCarthy-Morrogh), from Inish Beg House, Baltimore, County Cork, who was initially Eisenhower's chauffeur or driver, and later his personal secretary. A close wartime rapport had developed between them and a strong relationship evolved. That an actual affair ever occurred was never clear cut, but certain assumptions were made and have been believed.

Whatever about the imagined, the actual situation was one in which the German surprise attack succeeded and a huge salient, or bulge, was created, projecting into the American First Army's front line – and from which the battle got its name, the Battle of the Bulge.

Stunned and overwhelmed, some American sub-units surrendered and others withdrew. However, in many places trees were felled, craters blown into roads and, to the surprise of the Germans, brave resistance was offered – sufficient enough to slow the initial advances in the early hours and days of the battle. Along the weakly held, over-extended territory of the hilly, heavily forested Ardennes, the concentrated German tanks and infantry advanced, penetrating the Allied defences. So, at first, the attack proved successful, and German troops were ultimately to advance fifty miles into the Allied-held area. Their momentum was contested by the brave actions of stand-alone, small American units. American 28th Division had played a vital part in slowing the onslaught. Here and there, the Americans managed to plug gaps, strengthen road junction defences and reinforce areas, but it was mostly the faltering actions of a rearguard. The shattered Bastogne was one such area that became contested; the 101st Airborne and part of the

10th Armoured Division managed to make a stand there, only to become encircled and eventually surrounded. They held on tenaciously, putting up an obstinate defence, and so the Germans bypassed them and continued their advance, quickly reinforced. It was, however, a crucial road junction hub. Despite such feats, and despite contesting a massive assault and coping with a desperate and chaotic situation, it was not long before the now-isolated and fast-becoming-exhausted Allied defenders weakened.

Hitler succeeded in catching the Allies off guard. His last throw of the dice, his last chance to save the war, his last gamble, was proving to be stunningly effective. Moreover, his offensive was conducted in poor weather, neutralising the Allies' air superiority. Success, however, depended on the achievement of an out-and-out, unmitigated hammer blow against the Allies, allowing the Germans to capture fuel supplies intact, and all before the weather cleared.

Throughout this struggle, pandemonium and turmoil occurred in a historically deep European freeze. Icy rain, piercingly chill winds, sleet snow and bitterly cold conditions made simply staying alive difficult, let alone soldiering and trying to conduct operations. Tanks sliding off icy roads, attempting to dig fox holes in frozen ground, fog obscuring vision, routine logistical efforts being made exponentially more difficult – these are to name a few ways in which hardships became compounded. Soldiers also began to suffer from frostbite and trench foot – swollen feet characteristically turning blue-black, rendering even the removal of boots very difficult, or impossible. Many Americans, in particular, were not suitably clothed or kitted out for winter warfare and became casualties of the weather, which proved to be as much an enemy as the Germans were, with many being medevaced out of the theatre as a result.

Irish-American James Flanagan, 101st Airborne Division, had parachuted into the Normandy darkness, behind Utah Beach, prior to H-hour on D-Day. He was part of a group of paratroopers that captured a German command post in a farm complex near Ravenoville. Afterwards, an international news service photographed the group, with James Flanagan in the centre of the paratroopers, holding a Nazi flag. The photograph became one of the most widely distributed newspaper photographs taken from the events of 6 June. Three months later, involved in Operation Market Garden – a day jump this time – he was wounded in under twenty-four hours, when he came under mortar fire near Sint-Oedenrode and dozens of pieces of shrapnel entered his arms, ribs and legs. Two months later, he was returned to action and, within a week, was involved in the Battle of the Bulge in the Bastogne area.

Christmas Day, a particularly cold day, saw German Panzer tanks pushing through Allied lines near Sint-Oedenrode, penetrating their defences and overrunning positions. In response, American M4 Shermans and tank destroyers engaged the Panzers, while snipers picked off the accompanying infantry. An intensification of the exchange, however, saw an increase in incoming fire and James Flanagan's company had to retreat into the cover of a nearby wood. Running hard alongside him was an officer and between them was a large tree which suddenly exploded as it was hit directly by a German 88 shell, the force of which projected him through the air, where he landed in a stream. The force of his landing broke through the inch or so of ice, so now he was in trouble. Simultaneously, the American tank destroyers emerged out of the woods, swung around, and at near point-blank range fired at the vulnerable rear side of the Panzers. Unable to react fast enough – they were not as quick or responsive as the tank destroyers – none of the Panzers escaped the attack and the accompanying infantry were gunned down. Three feet deep in a freezing Belgian stream, James Flanagan quickly came down with frostbite. Removed from battle and hospitalised, he rejoined his platoon after two weeks and they were moved to the Alsace country. He survived the war, moved to Sacramento outside California, married a woman named Dorothy, and for more than fifty years had a varied career in aeronautics.

Only a few days before the incident on Christmas Day, the situation for the American First Army deteriorated rapidly, and finally the 'bulge' split the American 12th Army Group in two – to such an extent that the integrity of its command suffered and control was made extremely difficult. This was potentially problematic to the extent that Field Marshal Montgomery was tasked by Eisenhower to take command, at once, of all American forces on the northern flank of the bulge. That order put two American armies, the Ninth and the First, under Monty's command, along with his own 21st Army Group. Writing in his 1958 memoir, Montgomery stated:

The first thing to do was to see the battle on the northern flank as one whole, to ensure the vital areas were held securely and to create reserves for counter attack. I embarked on these measures. I put British troops under command of the Ninth Army to fight alongside American soldiers, and had that army take over some of the First Army front. I positioned British troops as reserves behind the First and Ninth Armies until such time as American reserves could be created. Slowly but surely the situation was held, and then finally restored. Similar action was taken on the southern flank of the bulge by Bradley with the Third (US) Army.

Monty also placed General Horrocks' XXX Corps behind the River Meuse, in the general area between Louvain and Namur, in order to prevent any German units crossing the Meuse. Lieutenant General Brian Horrocks' mother, Minna Moore, was the daughter of the Reverend J.C. Moore of Connor, County Antrim. It was XXX Corps that had to move quickly up the sixty-four-mile single route over the captured bridges to Arnhem as a part of Operation Market Garden. At its forefront was the Guards Armoured Division, commanded by Major General Allan Adair, consisting of roughly 13,000 men and 200 tanks. Leading them was the Irish Guards under the command of Lieutenant Colonel John Ormsby Evelyn 'Joe' Vandeleur. Montgomery, the architect of Operation Market Garden, as well as General Horrocks, Major General Adair and Lieutenant Colonel Vandeleur had strong Irish connections, and there were many other such associations among the men of the 82nd and 101st US airborne divisions, both rank and file and in command positions. Now they were all back battling at the Bulge.

An Allied containment and counter-measure strategy was worked out: pins were placed on map boards in various headquarters, units positioned on the ground and orders relayed. Now it was down to the on-ground commanders and soldiers to fight the fight. With the Allied troops now regrouped on either flank of the bulge, they began to fight back. On the northern flank of the bulge, American combat engineers blew up bridges, while on the southern flank American troops blocked road junctions to slow the advance. Two of the most important junctions were at St Vith and the aforementioned Bastogne. Here, the Americans had held on but were surrounded and bypassed by the Germans. However, as St Vith and Bastogne were important intersections of the road network in these areas, Allied possession of these territories blocked the German supply lines; for this reason, repeated attempts were made by the Germans to capture them. St Vith fell, but when the Germans demanded the surrender of the outnumbered and surrounded American troops in the town of Bastogne, Irish-American General Anthony McAuliffe replied to the ultimatum with the now-famed single-word response – 'NUTS'. He and his men continued to hold their ground, and the town, until they were relieved by the US 4th Armoured Division on 26 December.

The fighting continued unabated: underground with mines and counter-mines, overhead with tree bursts. The effect of accurate explosions from mortars and artillery detonating among the forests exacerbated their destructiveness, as the trees and branches splintered, adding to the mass of shrapnel slivers and fragments showering down with force on those cowering in their foxholes.

And then, another German shock. In fact, a shock within a shock. As Hitler had done with *Wacht am Rhein* ('Watch on the Rhine'), the successful surprise offensive into the Ardennes, Reichsmarschall Hermann Goering was now doing with Operation Bodenplatte (Baseplate) when, on New Year's Day 1945, nearly 1,000 Luftwaffe aircraft took off from forty airfields, targeting twelve British airfields in Belgium and Holland, and four American airfields in France. Surprise was achieved here too, as large formations of Luftwaffe *Staffeln* (squadrons) deployed together in one strike. Many among the Messerschmitt 109 pilots were new and inexperienced, having only flown solo for a few hours. Nevertheless, Goering was going all out. And it had its effect: Allied fighter and fighter bomber aircraft were destroyed on the ground or caught ('bounced') just as they were taking off. All told, around 150 Allied aircraft were destroyed and over 100 damaged. Few pilots were killed, however.

Many Luftwaffe fighter aircraft were brought down by anti-aircraft fire, both Allied and German, because Goering had refused, for reasons of operational security, to allow his own anti-aircraft defences to receive advance warning of Operation Bodenplatte. Also, having sprung their successful surprise hit-and-run raids, many Luftwaffe pilots lingered, continuing to attack, and delaying so long that Allied fighters from rear bases had time to scramble, get in the air and catch them as they were beginning to turn back to their bases. Those who escaped had, once again, to 'run the gauntlet' of their own anti-aircraft flak fire. Overall, around 270 aircraft were destroyed and over 50 aircraft damaged. The total number of Luftwaffe pilot casualties (dead, wounded and missing) was near 250. Goering achieved a surprise; however, he could barely claim a victory, losing more aircraft than they were able to replace. It was to be the final deathblow for the German Luftwaffe.

Meanwhile, back on the ground, the Allies continued to finalise the organisation of their troop dispositions; short of fuel, and having over-extended their supply lines, the German advance slowed, then halted. Montgomery ordered the British XXX Corps – Cork man John Stout, Irish Guards Armoured Division, was among them – into line to allow the Americans to reorganise for the counterattack. The situation was deadlocked – the Germans were not able to push forward and the Allies were not yet set to counterattack – so fierce fighting continued to fill the impasse. The deadly stalemate was only broken when the weather improved enough to allow the Allies to bring their advantage in air supremacy into play, pummelling German attack and supply lines to great effect. All along, the American artillery had played a huge role in supporting the infantry; now the full weight of Allied air support allowed Monty to move from the north and Patton to move from the south. The counter-offensive had begun.

The final phase of the battle had come into play. When the Allied counterattack ended, it was to see Germany's gamble – Hitler's final offensive – dissipate. His depleted forces were routed and retreated to their original positions, with 120,000 casualties (dead, wounded, missing and captured) and much of his war fighting assets, such as tanks, artillery and aircraft, destroyed. It had been a 'bloody nose', too, for the Americans, who suffered some 80,000 casualties and whose complacency in defending the line along the Ardennes – US General Omar Bradley's 'risk taking' in thinking the hilly, heavily forested terrain was likely to be considered unsuitable by the Germans – was severely punished.

The battle over, the physical contest decided, Field Marshal Montgomery was now engaged with the media against the background of a vexed question – his supposed scheming to have himself named as overall commander of the ground forces. Matters were not helped by the British media demanding this appointment, while the American media and public, only now learning that Montgomery had taken charge of the First and Ninth US Armies, deeply resented any possibility of this becoming a fixed position – as did their military. In his 1958 memoir, Montgomery said of the 7 January press conference, which he held on the subject of the battle:

> I was perturbed at this time about the sniping at Eisenhower, which was going on in the British press. So I sent a message to the Prime Minister and said that in my talk to British and American correspondents about the battle, I proposed to deal with the story of the battle. I would show how the whole Allied team rallied to the call and how team work saved a somewhat awkward situation. I suggested I should then put in a strong plea for Allied solidarity. Nothing must be done by anyone that tends to break down the team spirit. It is team work that pulls you through dangerous times. It is team work that wins battles. It is victories in battle that win wars.

The British Prime Minister agreed and said that what Montgomery proposed would be invaluable. Monty held the conference, of which many stories have been told, and from which many quotations have been taken out of context and published. Matters were not helped by a Nazi broadcast – a propaganda trick, blatant, deliberate and effective – whereby a German radio station, cleverly transmitting on a BBC wavelength, inaccurately reported that the Battle of Ardennes was saved from being an American First Army disaster thanks to Field Marshal Montgomery. This mischievous misinformation was believed, by the American media and troops, to be a real broadcast. US generals were angered, Churchill appalled, Montgomery distressed and worried.

There were bigger issues at hand, however. Fighting the battle had taken some six weeks. The Russians encroached ever closer to Germany's eastern frontier, and this was to be the cause of some political consequences – the countdown to war's end became more and more imminent.

3

THUNDERCLAP AND BOMBING THE BIG B

'Concentrated on killing' was how Audie Leon Murphy, from Texas and of Irish descent, described his whole being, and he had, through his circumstances, engaged in much killing – as a platoon leader, an America infantry lieutenant (battlefield commission), and even beforehand he was involved in combat situations where it had become necessary. Exposed to many instances of enemy hostility, it was imperative to fight back in order to survive or achieve the mission. There was no doubting, however, that he was very good at it. A sharp shot with a hunter's instinct for stalking prey, he was brave to a degree that was bold; he was a man of action, likely to seize the moment when others would not and tip the balance in many close-quarter small unit actions. He had a certain type of flair to his energy which he had already demonstrated in Italy – in Tunisia, Sicily and Anzio – bringing him notice and quick promotion to staff sergeant. On 15 August 1944, with the 15th Infantry Regiment, 3rd Division, he played a part in Operation Dragoon, which involved an invasion force of 70,000 hitting sixteen beaches along a forty-five-mile stretch of the Côte d'Azur near Marseilles and Nice; Murphy and the 15th Infantry Regiment came ashore close to St Tropez and Ramatuelle, at Yellow Beach. This military action was originally named Operation Anvil, which was due to coincide with Operation Overlord, the Allied landings at Normandy on D-Day, 6 June 1944, but a shortage of landing craft necessitated its postponement. Staff Sergeant Audie Murphy and his squad, when moving inland, came up against opposition from German machine-gun nests. He singlehandedly took out four of them, at one stage firing from the hip with a seized enemy machine gun – an action for which he was awarded the Distinguished Service Cross. He was to become one of the most highly decorated American combat soldiers of the Second World War, and he was off Irish descent. From a very humble, almost disadvantaged background, he was the seventh of twelve in a motherless family (she had died) struggling to survive. His father, a small farmer during the Depression, was frequently absent from the homestead and was eventually to desert his children. Dropping out of school, his rough upbringing and lack of a proper childhood made Audie grow up fast; he became quick-witted, with a certain sharpness of mind, and was quick to see and seize an opportunity. His 1942 enlistment papers, forged by his sister, falsely attested that he was eighteen years old, when in fact he was a year younger.

New Year's Day 1945 witnessed a surprise Luftwaffe attack on Allied airfields during the Battle of the Bulge, but it was also on this day that a second surprise was sprung: a German attack into northern Alsace, beyond the Vosges mountains. Both the assault on Ardennes and this Alsace advance were eventually overcome, but in the latter the Germans in the Colmar Pocket continued to hold out. On 26 January, the Allies were further exasperated when they once again failed to clear the Pocket. However, the day had its successes, a notable one involving the already twice-decorated Lieutenant Audie Murphy. While involved in defending against an attack from infantry and Panzer tanks near Riedwihr, Murphy, outnumbered and outgunned, jumped onto a disabled and burning American tank destroyer, and pinned down the advancing Germans while calling in artillery fire support; this lasted for an hour, and he only stopped when he ran out of ammunition. For this exceptional exploit, he was awarded the Medal of Honour. There were other such exploits, and he was justifiably awarded further decorations. He survived the war and afterwards became a celebrated Hollywood actor for twenty-one years, and was later a writer and singer of country music. The psychological effects of the war remained with him, however, and he became an advocate of publicly highlighting battle stress in the hope that others in need of support and treatment would receive it, and that the government would provide it.

From on-ground fighting to the bigger perspective of the aircrew in the skies, the war was fought and experienced from all angles. There were those generals, notably Commander-in-Chief of Bomber Command, Arthur Harris, and commander of the United States Army Air Force (USAAF) Carl Spaatz, who believed firmly in the cause of independent air power; they were also strong in the belief that the strategic objective could be achieved from the air alone, and therefore that land operations were unnecessary and costly risks. Instead, they wished to persist with, and indeed intensify, the aerial bombing of Germany. Operation Thunderclap was a long-term bombing campaign, grand in its scope, scale and intensity, which planned to strike German oil, industrial and transportation targets. The aim of this continual, saturated 'area bombing' was to drive Germany to a state of devastation – for them to become dispirited and depleted to such an extent that their surrender would not only be inevitable, but also come sooner. Seriously reduce Germany's capacity to make war and they would have to make peace. Both Harris and Spaatz were unconvinced and reluctant to divert their air assets to Operation Pointblank – a plan to hit transport networks in Northern France in advance of D-Day. By hitting railway junctions, stations, marshalling yards and bridges over the River Seine, it was hoped that the Allies would impede the reinforcement capability of the Germans in any effort to counter the D-Day invaders. General Eisenhower had to insist that Churchill follow the directive.

Vital air cover enabled the largest amphibious invasion in history, and was crucial to subsequent operations and engagements. Once the European offensive was well progressed and the German frontier in sight, the bombing campaign of Germany, maintained throughout the offensive, could resume once again to its fullest effect. The Allies, having seized and held terrain all the way from the northern French coastline to the German frontier, also controlled the skies above, because German fighter aircraft, with no airstrips below, could not set upon them. In addition, in 1944 the US P-51 Mustang fighter was rejuvenated by the refitting of a Rolls Royce Merlin engine (it was previously powered by the Allison engine) and so had a greater range and could now escort the B-17 Flying Fortress and B-24 Liberator bombers of the US Eighth and Ninth air forces for longer. Lastly, the Luftwaffe had lost so many aircraft and experienced pilots that air superiority was unquestionably with the Allies. What was left of their aircraft was in the hands of mostly young, inexperienced pilots who had little fuel available to them. One worry for the Allies, however, was the existence of the vastly superior German Luftwaffe Me 262 jet fighters and the potential production capacity for more of them before the war ended. The Me 262s and flak (anti-aircraft) defences over the target areas were ferocious.

Survival statistics were stark – a mere third of the US Eighth Air Force crews outlasted twenty-five missions; once the P-51 fighter was able to provide long-range escort over Germany, the figure rose to two-thirds. For pilots, co-pilots, engineers, bombardiers, navigators and machine gunners, there was a target for the number of missions completed before being made exempt from flying further missions – this was considered advisable when taking into account the statistical probability of being shot down and killed (or suffering severely from battle stress). For the RAF, it was thirty bombing missions; for the USAAF, initially, it was twenty-five – then it rose to thirty-five and beyond. The RAF flew only at night and undertook area bombings, while the USAAF conducted day-time bombing raids which were more precisely targeted. This 24-hour bombing over Germany saw heavy damage inflicted upon many German war material manufacturing facilities, and particularly to the heavily industrialised Ruhr valley oil refineries. Aircraft and ball bearing production plants were among the targeted priorities, the latter because they were a vital part in every mechanical device and armament used in wartime. As a result, at times, the Germans' manufacturing of ball bearings was reduced, but important reserves were received, from neutral Switzerland and especially Sweden, until production resumed in dispersed plants.

Massive numbers of bombers assembled to further concentrate their efforts, and for reasons of security and protection. Huge waves of bombers – in the high hundreds, up to and even exceeding one thousand – pummelled targets in Germany unrelentingly, day and night. Many aircraft were shot down with their crews killed, wounded, missing or captured. Fatality rates remained high, even for the night-flying RAF, where it was estimated that it was as high as over 40 per cent.

Many men from Ireland – north and south – were part of the RAF Bomber Command crews. Some among them were: Jimmy Burns, County Kildare; John 'Sean' Drumm, County Offaly; Worth Newenham, County Cork; Liam Lawn, County Donegal; Fred O'Donovan, Jim Redmond and

Denis Murnane, County Dublin; James 'Paddy' Forsythe, County Belfast; John McFarland, County Derry; and Martin Charters, County Down. In addition, there were many Irish, and many with strong connections to Ireland, among the pilots of the bombers' fighter escorts. This was evident, even from early on in the war, with the strong Irish participation with 'the few' in the Battle of Britain, aces among them. Much of the RAF ground crews were Irish, as were many RAF doctors, dentists and chaplains; overall, there was also a high representation of Irish throughout command levels.

Most of the damage and death to Allied bombers was inflicted by flak. Curtains of exploding shells were fired up into the skies, day and night, ahead of bombers' flight trajectory, for them to fly into. There were many near misses, and differing degrees of damage caused – but also deadly direct hits. The flak fire was often terrifying; its impact was described as sounding like a tin roof in a hail storm. Even when it didn't strike directly, the outside air compressions from its explosions buffeted the aircraft – a kind of kinetic turbulence that was troubling. John McFarland, from County Derry, a Stirling bomber navigator, tells of a different danger, one he himself experienced on the night of 18 April 1944, over the North Sea – that of the German night fighter. The night fighters stalked their prey from behind and below, positioning themselves under the bomber, getting in close, and when an opportunity presented itself they engaged at an upward firing angle, damaging or directly blowing their target out of the sky. When McFarland's bomber was attacked, they were hit badly and going down. The pilot ordered a bail out while he and the engineer kept the aircraft in flight. John McFarland was the first out of the hatch. Four of the crew got out of the aircraft but the rear gunner's parachute did not open. Three men did not even get out of the aircraft: the pilot, the engineer and the mid-upper gunner. Floating down, John hoped he would not land in water, because he could not swim. He landed in the middle of a field around midnight and was found and sheltered by a Danish farming family, who hid him in a barn. Unfortunately, word got out through schoolchildren, who were excitedly aware of John and his two colleagues – both of whom were similarly being sheltered nearby – and they were all captured by the Germans. They were sent to the Stalag Luft III prisoner-of-war camp for captured aircrew in Zagan, Poland, and from which, a month previously, there had been a major breakout. Fifty of the seventy-four escapees, when captured, were executed by the Gestapo on Hitler's orders. In January 1945, as the Russians approached, the prisoners of war were marched west; the column, mistakenly believed to be escaping German troops, was strafed by two British aircraft and twenty men were killed. They were eventually freed by the British a few months later, at war's end.

In March 1945, after twenty-one operational flights, Denis Peter Murnane, Dubliner and RAF bombardier, was also shot down. Having parachuted and landed safely, he was captured by a man from the Luftwaffe with perfect English; he had learned it at the internment camp in the Curragh, County Kildare. Fellow Dubliner Jim Redmond, an RAF tail gunner, described the reality of night-time encounters with enemy fighter aircraft in *Witnesses to War*, an RTE documentary, 'People forget it was dark. Things were happening so fast. He [the German fighter aircraft] is moving at speed, you are moving at speed; it's pitch black. It was a matter of seconds; by the time you picked him up, he was almost gone.'

John Joseph 'Sean' Drumm, Tullamore, County Offaly, was also an air crew gunner with Bomber Command; he flew thirty-two operational missions from 1943 to 1945. Prior to that, he was in the Irish Air Corps (1939–43). In 1942–3 there was a large exodus from the Irish Air Corps into the RAF. Another gunner, Martin Charters, Killealeagh, County Down, flew in Halifax and Lancaster bombers with Bomber Command. He was active in bombing raids over Germany, including 800 bomber raids into the Ruhr valley and a 1,000 bomber raid on the city of Cologne. His crew was one of two picked for special operations, which involved flying very low, to avoid detection on their way to their target, going in only twenty feet or so over the North Sea. He was also involved in raids on Nuremberg in February 1944, where ninety-two aircraft were shot down.

Liam Lawn, a flight engineer from County Donegal, flew in Lancaster bombers, taking part in dozens of bombing raids over France and Germany. Returning from a raid over France, his Lancaster bomber did not make it to home base; after sustaining damage, it crashed less than a mile from the airfield. Of the seven crew, three were killed. The other four, including Liam, were seriously injured. He spent several months in hospital, but was back flying again in December 1944, whereupon he successfully completed several more missions, surviving the war. At the outbreak of the Second World War, Worth Newenham's father impressed upon him the importance of enlisting in a 'good regiment', but Worth insisted on joining the RAF. Worth was from Coolmore, Carrigaline, County Cork. He trained in Australia and Canada, eventually graduating to pilot a Lancaster bomber with 106 Squadron. Between October 1944 and May 1945, he flew thirty missions over Germany and Norway, once barely making it back after a fierce attack by a German Ju 88. Worth Newenham survived the war.

Air Commodore James Roy 'Paddy' Forsythe, a pilot from Belfast, flew a Lancaster bomber with 625 Squadron, joining the RAF after the bombing raids on Belfast in April and May 1941. It was estimated that as many as 1,000 civilians were killed in these bombings, poorly directed efforts to hit the city's important sea port and shipyard and its refineries and power plants, to cause havoc to their aircraft and textiles industries. He trained in the US under the 'Arnold Scheme', a bilateral agreement between Britain and the US which saw thousands of RAF pilots trained at airfields in the southeast – Georgia, in Paddy's case. On 13 February 1945, 625 Squadron, with Flight Lieutenant Paddy Forsythe among them, attacked the German city of Dresden in Saxony, southeastern Germany, one of the most controversial bombing raids – in fact, there were three separate attacks within forty-eight hours – of the entire war. The aim was to hit the railway marshalling yards, in order to wreck the German rail transport network there, but also to assist the Russian Red Army, who were preparing to attack the city from the east. The effect of the raid was intense, aided, apparently, by unusually strong winds which, it was claimed, blew flames into the city itself; tens of thousands were killed in a devastating series of fires. The head of Bomber Command, Air Chief Marshal Arthur Harris, was heavily criticised for the bombing of Dresden and bombing raids on other German cities intended to weaken civilian will for continued German participation in the war. Whether the Dresden winds gave rise to the firestorm, further exacerbating the destruction and devastation of the city, has been an issue over the years, many believing Harris was to blame – though it was in fact Churchill's responsibility. Paddy Forsythe also took part in the dropping of food supplies to the starving population of the Netherlands during their 'Hungerwinter'.

Debate has raged regarding justifications for the 'terror bombing' of Dresden, with its beautiful baroque architecture, which had seen a large influx of refugees swelling its number of inhabitants. It has been said that it had no real military targets and wondered whether, as it was so late in the war, the attack was really necessary. Some say its grim necessity was payback for the bombing of Coventry earlier in the war, and that, mindful of the post-war situation with the Russians, it was important to show them what Bomber Command could do.

Along with Irish-born members of the RAF, there were those of Irish descent serving both in the RAF and the USAAF. One such RAF participant was New York-born Joseph Charles 'Big Joe' McCarthy, who served with the Royal Canadian Air Force (RCAF) in Bomber Command during the Second World War, famously flying with 617 Squadron in the second wave of Operation Chastise, the 'Dam Buster' raid of 1943. By this time, he was a well-experienced pilot, having participated in thirty bombing sorties over Germany, including three over Berlin.

Bombing 'The Big B' (Berlin) was a hazardous undertaking. Its air defences included six purpose-built, enormous, reinforced-concrete flak towers; on the roof of each tower was a battery of eight five-inch guns and multiple-barrelled, quick-firing 'pom pom' cannons. The crews on these towers would vigorously empty their stock of ammunition into the skies during Allied bombing raids. Similar examples of these eight-foot-thick walled air defences remain in existence in Vienna today.

In all, more than 55,000 RAF Bomber Command crew were killed in the war. The fatality rate, 44 per cent, was high, but, then again, its crews were employed in difficult and dangerous missions: flak, night fighters, bad weather, mechanical faults, sometimes just bad luck – or a combination of all – could lead to their deaths. Pilot Officer James Gerald 'Jimmy' Burns, son of Thomas and Stella Burns, who were from the Curragh, County Kildare, was killed in action, at 23 years of age, on 4 April 1945, when his Halifax bomber aircraft MZ460 from RAF Breighton exploded mid-air near the target area in the vicinity of Hamburg.

Many others had close calls, near misses and fortunate escapes, managing to bring badly stricken aircraft back to bases and airfields – or otherwise making successful emergency landings in fields or ditching in 'the drink' and being rescued. For others, however, probability came calling: if you court danger often enough, it can have its consequences. Every time they took to the air, aircrew were taking their life in their hands. Sometimes a large proportion of bombers and crews in a squadron might not return from a mission. In Dubliner Denis Murnane's 4 Group, 51 Squadron, only ten out of twenty-one bombers and crew came back safely after one particularly hazardous night.

The perilous pursuit of bombing raid targets in enemy territory saw many Allied bombers shot down and their aircrew members killed. One who was wounded was Fred O'Donovan, from Drumcondra, Dublin, who served as a wireless operator/air gunner top turret on a Lancaster bomber. His wounds, however, were received as a result of friendly fire – he got shrapnel in his knee when a nearby USAAF crew cleared their guns into his aircraft. Sent to Long Kesh in Northern Ireland (then the site of a military hospital), he volunteered for a new unit once recuperated – the RAF Missing Research and Enquiry Service (MRES), which was active between 1944 and 1953. The MRES was set up to trace the 42,000 RAF personnel who were listed as 'missing, believed killed'. Highly successful, the MRES was expanded and able to account for over two-thirds of the missing personnel. These men were found, identified and reinterred in Commonwealth War Graves Commission plots. The work allowed families the comfort of knowing what happened to their loved ones, affording them the dignity to finally grieve. Summating its value, Fred O'Donovan stated, 'It was the best, most fulfilling and honourable thing I did in my entire life. I felt what I was doing was something so right, as it was so important for the families of those RAF men missing since even as far back as Dunkirk.' O'Donovan joined the RAF because he believed he was defending Ireland – that Hitler was a world problem. An excellent soccer player, he was picked for the RAF XIs, representing them throughout Europe. A scout approached him at one of the matches and he was subsequently selected for Arsenal, but the very same day he was told he had tuberculosis. As an MRES search officer, Fred O'Donovan was despatched, post-invasion, to places throughout France and Belgium where aircraft were believed to have crashed. This work involved on-ground investigations: interviewing local town mayors, gendarmerie, priests, and anyone else likely to have had any morsel of information that would help. The identification of airmen who had died was often assisted by the smallest of details: initials on a personal artefact, a serial number, or maybe a name on the laundry label of an item of clothing. Painstaking, often harrowing, it was nonetheless richly rewarding work. It even had its surprises: one day Fred found a 'live body', so to speak – a 'downed airman' alive and well and very happy in his circumstance.

Seeking assistance one day in the newly established Irish Red Cross Hospital at Saint-Lô, Fred O'Donovan met who he believed was the caretaker, an Irishman named Sam. They had a pleasant chat and Fred thought no more of it. Then, some months later, he was requested to attend a function in the British Embassy in Paris; as he was Irish himself, it was thought he might assist the embassy staff in playing host to the invited guest, an Irish writer whom they regarded as rather shy, reticent and quiet spoken. When he was subsequently introduced to the writer, a Mr Samuel Beckett, Fred O'Donovan immediately recognised him as the 'caretaker' he had met at the Irish Red Cross Hospital at Saint-Lô.

He was also involved in an investigation looking into the whereabouts of the bodies of 'the fifty': those escapees from the prisoner-of-war camp at Stalag Luft III in Zagan, Poland, who were later the subject of the 1963 epic Hollywood film *The Great Escape*. It was somewhat coincidental that his work brought him into a search for the aircrew escapees, because, although not one of 'the fifty', his own brother Sean, also in the British army, was a bit of an escape artist himself.

The RAF and USAAF were helping to extend the Allied offensive eastward while, below them, the ground forces battled towards Berlin – and the unrelenting Germans fought them every step of the way. However, as Frederick the Great said, 'He who defends everything, defends nothing.' The Germans had been defending everywhere in Europe – now the Germans had only to defend Germany. Breaking into Nazi Germany, seizing tactically advantageous territories, cities and towns, meant there was still much fighting to be done, and German resistance was likely to be fierce.

The difficulty for the Germans was that they had now to defend their western and eastern frontiers, and to put up a defence on German soil. The ground war was to be fought on German land, on both borders at once, and against huge, well-equipped armies. Their worn-out army was greatly reduced in number, ill provisioned and short of supplies; transport was scarce, they were very low on armaments and ammunition, and had practically run out of fuel. Operation Herbstnebel ('Autumn Mist'), Hitler's last throw of the dice in the Ardennes, was a needless squander of valuable military assets, in a hopeless offensive, at a time when he desperately needed to consolidate a strong defence. As a result, his strategic reserve, already committed, was gone, and he chose to reconstitute it with the Volkssturm, a national militia made up of old men and young boys. He further dissipated his forces by dispatching the 6th SS Panzer Division to defend oil fields in Hungary, west of Lake Balaton, which easily fell prey to the advancing Russians. Finally, he had garrisoned territory in the Courland Peninsula, in Latvia, with 200,000 troops; he was carried by the notion to 'never give up land' and these troops were surrounded, sitting out the war instead of breaking out and coming to Germany's aid.

For all their shortfalls – their depleted readiness, their deficient defensive capabilities, their lack of first line crack troops – Hitler was determined to make a stand; the Germans still retained a formidable fighting capacity and the Allies had yet to cross the Rhine.

4
FORCING THE RHINE

The supporting artillery was cacophonous and the Allied assault troops were on the better end of the barrage. Despite advancing under the hail of this protective fire in amphibious, tracked Buffalo transporters over the Rhine River, the Allied troops would have been foolish not to be afraid amid this uproar. The Germans, in their machine-gun nests, mortar pits and strong points, were prepared and responding with lethal fire. For the attackers there was a battle plan, a timed and co-ordinated sequence of actions to be executed, a detailed and impressive offensive, but there was no certainty. There was a commander's intent, but no actual script; there was a scheme, but no predetermined narrative. This was war, and each battle had its own unfolding events and episodes. There was noise, a lot of noise, an unsettling amount of noise. There was the unknown, there was doubt, there was probability and the implausible. There was fear because there was danger. The Allied situation was hazardous and precarious; they were exposed to the likelihood of harm or death; shrapnel slivers from exploding mortars hit the assault craft while machine-gun rounds were also finding their mark. There was vivid risk and peril, but there was also compelling courage – there had to be. After all, the Allies were finally forcing the Rhine and breaking into Nazi Germany.

The Rhine River was a forbidding natural defensive feature and the prospect of having to cross it while a prepared enemy, a proven foe, was on the opposite bank was fearsome. Wide, deep and dangerous, it was an intrinsic impediment, an abundant barrier obstructing the Allies from progressing their advance into Germany proper. Flowing north from Switzerland, fed by glaciers, and emptying into the North Sea, the broad, unfordable Rhine River had proven a significant and insurmountable stumbling block to invasion from the west over the centuries. It was no less an obstruction in March 1945, with all of its thirty-one bridges destroyed by the retreating German army. The Allies knew that by overcoming this huge physical hurdle, it would force a change in the German mindset; the Germans would finally be confronted with the reality of having to face and acknowledge defeat. It was both that difficult and that simple.

And yet Allies succeeded in forcing the Rhine at three different points – Remagen, Oppenheim and Wesel – while employing three different approaches. The crossing at Remagen was achieved when a still-standing, largely unattended railway bridge that failed to blow up was opportunistically seized on 7 March; the route through Oppenheim was exploited by way of a bold, clandestine, largely unopposed infiltration-type river crossing on 23 March; the crossing at Wesel was breached by a large-scale, powerful, expertly executed, all-out river assault on 24 March.

Early morning on 7 March, a US spotter plane pilot looking for opportunity artillery targets unexpectedly noticed that the Ludendorff railway bridge at Remagen was intact; German soldiers were still retreating across it. The pilot's astonishing discovery was rapidly relayed, via radio, through the various communication centres in the chain of command; the unit in closest proximity to it was ordered to use all force necessary to take possession of it. The task, apart from the obvious one of engaging (and being shot by) enemy forces, implied the possibility that, should the Germans try to blow the bridge up, then everyone in the Allied attack force would very likely be blown to smithereens. Emergency demolition charges were indeed set on the bridge, and German engineers, on seeing the advancing US platoon, twisted the key on the plunger unit – instantaneously, two deafening explosions erupted, but amazingly the bridge structure remained intact. Zigzagging, ducking, weaving, flat-out running, the US platoon made their way forward, aware of being under fire and that the German engineers were desperately twisting the key and pushing down on the plunger. Passing the TNT-packed demolition charges, the platoon used wire cutters, snapping the ties connecting the charges to the bridge and letting each fall into the Rhine without detonating.

Moving swiftly forward, the Allies advanced off the bridge and into nearby high ground, holding the position. They were exhilarated beyond expectation; it was a real surprise to have claimed such a magnificent prize. Even though the rugged hinterland, with poor roads beyond, was far from ideal for further exploitation, and its remoteness would not pass a planner's criteria as 'strategic', suddenly, because the Allies had possession of an intact bridge, it was immediately of critical import. Both the Americans and Germans rushed troops, tanks and vehicles to the toehold bridgehead. High praise from an ecstatic US high command was mirrored by blame and fault-finding by Hitler; four German lieutenants were court martialled and executed, and Field Marshal Gerd von Rundstedt, as commander OB West, was dismissed and removed (replaced by Field Marshal Albert Kesselring). Four other German generals swiftly followed. The Germans made desperate efforts to recapture or destroy the bridge; the Americans were equally determined to develop the bridgehead and defend the bridge. The Germans attempted to bomb it from the air using Me 262 bomber jet fighters, Stuka dive bombers, artillery, frogmen (scuba divers) and even by floating mines down the river – all to no avail. A dozen V-2 rockets were also used by the Germans, but only one landed anywhere near the bridge. Meanwhile the Americans pushed as many troops and tanks (including their new Pershing tank, with its 75mm gun) across it as possible, to hurriedly consolidate their new-found opportunity. Masses of American anti-aircraft guns were put into position and a huge concentration of flak greeted any approaching enemy aircraft, many of which were shot down. Over the coming days, American engineers worked feverishly to strengthen the bridge and construct pontoon bridges nearby, used to get more troops, equipment and supplies across the river. They were to support the now five-miles-deep by fifteen-miles-wide fragile bridgehead. With the fighting ongoing and fierce, suddenly the weakened Ludendorff Bridge, of itself, collapsed, killing thirty and wounding seventy, roughly, of the US engineers working on it. Nonetheless, the flow of men and materials continued to cross the Rhine River at remote Remagen, the bridgehead expanding to ten miles deep and twenty five miles wide on the east side of the Rhine. Only it was very much in the wrong place.

The Allies' main effort was a well-planned, elaborate attack in the north, near Wesel. Beyond this crossing was the major objective of the industrialised

Ruhr valley; on the far side of the Ruhr was good traversable terrain leading straight to Berlin. Combining the depth of planning from D-Day and the lessons learned from Operation Market Garden, Operation Plunder and its associated airborne element, Operation Varsity, were designed to boldly break into Germany, beginning the fully orchestrated drive into the heart of the Third Reich. This would bring Montgomery's 21st Army Group to Berlin – and Monty very much wanted to be the first Allied general making his way into the German capital.

However, so too did US General Patton – and he also wanted to cross the Rhine River before Montgomery. Patton actually succeeded in doing so when, on 23 March at Oppenheim, six battalions of American troops stealthily slipped across the Rhine in assault boats at 10.30 p.m., catching the Germans unawares, encountering minimal opposition, and stealing a march on Monty. Quickly thereafter, they brought tanks across on ferries and utilised a floating bridge, establishing a five-mile-deep bridgehead within twenty-four hours.

Further north, Montgomery was busily involved in the co-ordination of artillery and aerial bombardments – the correct sequencing of the many moving parts of Operations Plunder and Operation Varsity. Additionally, he was hosting an inopportune visit from Prime Minister Winston Churchill, who selfishly wanted to come and view the Allies forcing the Rhine for himself.

Operation Plunder and Operation Varsity had all the weight of some six months' planning behind it – begun in October, immediately after the reverse suffered in Operation Market Garden. The long-awaited 'Bouncing of the Rhine' involved the careful building of supply bases, the massing together of men and fighting material, the conducting of aerial and other reconnaissance, the amassing and analysis of intelligence, and the hosting of briefings. Pent-up preparations could now give way to concerted action; a brutal artillery barrage was a significant statement of intent, its pragmatic effect to soften up the enemy defences. Thousands of artillery guns concentrated their formidable might on to pre-selected targets, their firepower coherently delivering vast quantities of explosive ordnance shells, pummelling enemy positions on the eastern shore. Their ruthlessly synchronised 'fall of shot' struck hard and forcefully, striking fear into the psyche of the defenders.

It effectively disorientated the enemy, buckling the German defensive line, and with this their determination to defend. The Allied attack plan was all about the delivery of overwhelming momentum in order to achieve rapid dominance. The German defenders knew what was coming, but were powerless to prevent it. Neither were they taken by surprise regarding where it had come from; Monty had made no attempts at deception. His build-up of forces was well signalled by the use of smoke screens, which obstructed his precise preparations for at least a fortnight. The Germans' response was to mass their forces in the area, holding their armoured reserve to the rear. This pulling in of resources and reserves, especially armoured ones, stretched their defensive line along the Rhine further south, thereby aiding the Americans in finding gaps to exploit.

The numbers involved in the Rhine crossing operation was half that of D-Day – and less than half with regards to resources – but even given this fact, it is clear that Operation Varsity and Operation Plunder were very large undertakings. Indeed, the Rhine River was the last major hurdle to outright victory. The Allies had some ninety divisions; the Germans, nominally, had sixty – in reality, they had about half that, as many of their units were understrength. The standard recommended ratio of attackers to defenders when undertaking an offensive is 3:1; the ratio was upheld in this instance, though the Allies were also vastly superior in terms of equipment and armaments.

Some historical analysis tends to gloss over the achievement of the Rhine River crossing, arguably because it was so convincingly carried out. But it was arguably far more difficult an undertaking than is popularly apparent. Kevin Myers, Irish journalist and author, has said of the crossing in his 2016 Kinsale Lecture on Irish participation in the British Army during the Second World War:

> the Rhine crossing of 25 March, 1945 was second only in combat bloodiness – for the Irish anyway – to the D-Day landings. Nearly fifty Irishmen died in this operation, including two Irish doctors, Captain Patrick O'Flynn and Captain Gordon Sheill, MC, both from the south. From D-Day to VE Day, 850 Irishmen in the British army were killed in the liberation of North Western Europe. Almost half of them – well over 400 – were from the 26 counties. Nearly 650 Irishmen died in the land battles to free Italy, slightly over half from

Éire, and when the European war was finished, the Far East awaited. Nearly 300 southern Irishmen died with the British army in the liberation of Malaya and Burma.

Charles Whiting, in the 2002 edition of *Bounce the Rhine*, informs us, 'the opposition could still cause plenty of casualties from their dug in positions. When the Ulstermen (1st Battalion, Royal Ulster Rifles 1/RUR) started to count heads that day, they discovered they had lost sixteen officers and 243 other ranks, nearly a third of the battalion.'

One among the fatalities that day was Major Kenneth Herbert Donnelly, Rathgar, Dublin, who was shot by a sniper. He had landed at Landing Zone U3 and come under a very heavy volume of fire from nearby houses. Indeed, throughout landing zones U1 to U3, south-east of Ringenberg, there was stronger opposition than expected, with heavy anti-aircraft fire, armoured cars and self-propelled guns causing a number of casualties. The 25-year-old major from Rathgar had been commissioned into the Royal Ulster Rifles prior to the outbreak of war, on 26 January 1939; he had embarked with the BEF, where he was reported wounded – 'injured on the continent', according to a telegram received by his family. It was a superficial bullet wound to the back of the head and after receiving medical attention at an advanced dressing station, he continued fighting. Eventually outnumbered, outgunned and out-manoeuvred, the BEF were forced to retreat at Dunkirk; Donnelly was a part of an orderly withdrawal on board a naval destroyer ship prior to the arrival of the small craft flotilla.

Between 1941 and mid-1944, Donnelly, along with his battalion, partook in increasingly intensive training for the invasion of Europe. One such street-fighting course, on a bomb site in London, saw Donnelly jump from a wall, breaking both ankles, after which he spent a considerable term in the Royal Masonic Hospital in London. Recovered, he was among 'The Rifles', who were part of the Air Landing Brigade, 6th Airborne Division. They were used as glider airborne reinforcements, landing slightly north of Ranville, near Caen, on the evening of D-Day. They took up defensive positions on the invasion bridgehead's eastern flank, protecting it against counterattacks from the German 21st Panzer Division. From mid-June until mid-August, they were involved in actions which pivoted the huge might of the invasion force swinging eastwards towards Paris. Withdrawn via the Mulberry 'B' harbour – an artificial harbour – at Arromanches, he returned to England on 1 September 1944, and was to enjoy a number of days leave with family and fellow colleagues involved in the war, comrades in arms like Bob Sheridan, Ronnie Wilson, Robin Crockett, Tom Fitzgerald, Robin Rigby, Huw Wheldon and Medical Officer Dai Rees. Promoted to acting major on 30 December 1944, he was involved when the 6th Airborne Division was called into action during the Battle of The Bulge, to shore up the northern flank. Their involvement saw them face the 11th Panzer and Panzer Lehr divisions in the area around Celles; thereafter, from Rocheforte, they advanced southeastwards towards Ortheuville, until the 'bulge' was satisfactorily suppressed, whereupon they were withdrawn back to Wiltshire, England. Departing England in the hours of darkness early on 24 March, Major Kenneth Donnelly, having survived the war thus far, was unfortunately not destined to survive much further. He is buried in Reichswald Forest War Cemetery.

With the campaign swinging in the Allies favour, it was crucial to maximise the momentum gained. Using all his battle-fighting and battle-winning experiences, Montgomery had once again applied his assiduity towards building up the maximum possible number of men and materials. He sought overwhelming power and to be in control of as much as he could, because he knew that, in battle, unplanned things can happen, events change fast, you can be knocked off balance easily, situations stall or accelerate, and outcomes are far from guaranteed. The challenge of the Rhine River crossing was demanding but manageable, if he could keep risk-taking to a minimum and keep focused on practical fighting issues. Monty's confidence was high and compelling. His preparations were painstaking and designed to squeeze the soul and spirit out of the defenders.

With the sustained and ferocious artillery bombardment ongoing, it was time to press forward with the ground forces' cross-river assault. The first into the fray was the 51st Highland Division setting out for Rees. Next, the lead elements of the Special Services 'Commando' Brigade began their attack. Because of the differing river widths at their respective locations, the former took two-and-a-half minutes to cross, the latter four. Further waves of assaulting troops, from the 15th Scottish Division and the 30 and 75 US divisions, joined them at intervals. Perhaps its simplicity suggests it was an unadventurous plan, but there was plenty of excitement for those actually involved in the well-executed manoeuvre – particularly for those 'first in', as they took that fatalistic first step into the dark, fast-flowing, swirling, wide river waters to be ferried to the far bank where a hostile foe awaited them. Excitement enough for one lifetime, but many had been in action before and had seen friends fall.

Taking them there was the Buffalo amphibious tracked vehicle, another variant from the highly unorthodox range of Hobart's Funnies. Major General Sir Percy Hobart's father was from Dublin, his mother from County Tyrone; he was also known as 'Hobo'. Attending the Staff College, Camberley, in 1923, he recognised the predominance of tank warfare and volunteered to be transferred to the Royal Tank Corps. In 1934, Hobart became brigadier of the first permanent armoured brigade in Britain. Due to his 'unconventional' ideas about armoured warfare, he retired from the army in 1940 and joined the Home Guard. When Churchill discovered what had happened, Hobart was re-enlisted into the army and put in command of the 79th Armoured Division. His sister Betty, a widow, married Field Marshal Montgomery, who informed General Eisenhower of his need to build specialised beach obstacle-clearing tank-type vehicles. Under Hobart's supervision, direction and leadership, the 79th created a range of modified tank designs, collectively nicknamed by the US soldiers as 'Hobart's Funnies', which were used to great effect during the Normandy landings and the advance inland across Northwestern Europe.

At 2 a.m., the men and war-fighting equipment of General Sir Miles Christopher Dempsey's 2nd Army followed. General Dempsey enjoyed a close relationship with Montgomery. He commanded the British 2nd Army on D-Day and up to this point – he commanded them all the way across Northwestern Europe. A descendent of a powerful clan in Offaly and Laois, his family was originally 'O'Dempsey', one of whom built the monastery at Monasterevin in 1179. Terence O'Dempsey was knighted in the field in Kilternan, County Limerick, by Robert Devereux, 2nd Earl of Essex, in May 1589; he later became Viscount Clanmaliere and Baron Philipstown. He was loyal to the Catholic King James II, and as a result lost all his lands in 1691. Dempsey's branch of the family then left Ireland for Cheshire and are recorded in Liverpool by 1821. In 1945, Miles Dempsey married Viola O'Reilly, the youngest daughter of Captain Percy O'Reilly of Coolamber, County Westmeath.

Once the artillery barrages ceased, and prior to the main body crossing the river, 200 Lancaster bombers from RAF Bomber Command had been brought into action alongside 1,500 American B-17s (Flying Fortress); they unloaded their bombs on Luftwaffe bases and other high-priority targets such as the town of Wesel itself, which was almost completely flattened.

Irish participation – north and south – in the RAF's Bomber Command, had, by this stage in the war, already been long established. The very first RAF bomber pilot to be shot down and killed in 1939 was Willie Murphy from Cork. His navigator, Larry Slattery, from Thurles, County Tipperary, became the longest-serving 'British' prisoner of war (POW) of the war. Over the course of the war, some 250 men from southern Ireland died while fighting with Bomber Command.

Interestingly, its commander since 1937, and during the first eight months of the war, was Cork-born Air Chief Marshal Sir Edgar Ludlow-Hewitt, who, after being educated at the Royal Military Academy at Sandhurst, served with the Royal Irish Rifles. Having learned to fly, he was appointed to the Royal Flying Corps in August 1914, the predecessor to the Royal Air Force. Highly decorated by war's end, he had been promoted to the rank of Brigadier General. When the RAF came into being on 1 April 1918, he became the General Officer Commanding the Training Division; he held a number of key appointments following from this, and, in 1937, he was promoted to Air Chief Marshal, becoming the new commander of RAF Bomber Command. He was tasked to prepare it for the coming war. He eagerly undertook the task of expanding the bomber fleet, numerically; he also arrived at the belief that the standards of night flying and navigation needed to be raised and that vulnerability to daytime operations needed to be addressed. To rectify these deficiencies, he requested that more Operational Training Units be established. The Air Ministry did not share his concerns, feeling that monies spent on improvements to the number of pilots trained was better spent on expanding the quality of operational aircraft and crews – so he was sacked. There was, however, a subsequent realisation of the merits of his proposals; Sir Arthur Harris ('Bomber' Harris) was to later comment, 'Without the policy of Ludlow's, the dog would have eaten its own tail to hurting point within a few weeks, and would have been a dead dog beyond all hope of recovery within a few months. Ludlow-Hewitt saved the situation – and the war – at his own expense.'

Leaving the RAF in November 1945, Ludlow-Hewitt was to hold the rank of Air Chief Marshal longer than anyone. Appointed as Chairman of the Board of the College of Aeronautics, he retired from there in 1958. He died fifteen years later, at 87 years of age, in 1973. The cumulative efforts of all three wartime commanders of Bomber Command, air chief marshals Ludlow-Hewitt, Sir Charles Portal and Sir Arthur Harris, had developed the usefulness of this RAF air asset, now benefitting Montgomery in his operation to force the Rhine. Their bombing was accurate and effective, it neutralised much of the resistance, deterring and incapacitating the enemy – so much so that the Allies secured a foothold with few casualties. By then, the 79th and 30th divisions were pouring across the east bank of the Rhine while engagements were ongoing inland.

One such encounter saw then-Major, later Colonel, Sir Freddy Pile commanding a squadron of the 1st Royal Tank Regiment. Frederick 'Freddy' Pile was the son of General Sir Frederick Pile, who served concurrently and commanded Britain's anti-aircraft defence all through the war. He was also the grandson of Sir Thomas Devereux Pile, who had been Lord Mayor of Dublin 1900–1. Major Freddy Pile, having crossed the Rhine near Wesel, proceeded between Borken and Stadtlohn along a roadway amid thickly wooded terrain and was ambushed by a well-positioned and large enemy force, which had placed anti-tank guns to fire directly down the road while under excellent cover of dense woodland. From each flank, Panzerfausts (anti-tank shoulder-fired weapons) poured in at them. Three tanks were hit, two lit up in flames immediately. Black smoke bellowed and visibility became seriously impaired. Pile was ordered to withdraw and regroup for a night attack.

With an infantry company from the 2nd Battalion Devonshire Regiment and fourteen tanks, Pile set off down the road again at 1 a.m., managing to squeeze by the two still-burning action tanks that had previously been knocked out. Using incendiary ammunition from the machine guns of his lead tanks, Pile secured both flanks of the road; their fires set the woodlands alight and orange red flames quickly engulfed the enemy positions. Shot up and burnt up, the ambushers' will wavered and then cracked. By early morning, the tank squadron and accompanying 'Red Devon' infantry had not only forced through the ambush site, but had taken the bridge at Stadtlohn and the town of Ahaus beyond. Pile was awarded an immediate Military Cross.

A certain degree of disillusionment was beginning to take hold among the exhausted but still-resilient Wehrmacht. They were encouraged by their performance at Arnhem, but the resounding defeat of their last-ditch effort to strike for Antwerp and split the Allied army in two in the Battle of the Bulge had reversed any such optimism. Their efforts to stall for time in order to develop a secret weapons programme and produce the hoped-for 'Wonder Weapon', which Hitler was promising, was now less and less likely to ever be achieved. Germany was running out of men, materials, time and space; the war had reached German soil. The last great Allied assault of the Second World War was at hand and, with the battle begun, Montgomery's eagerness to break into Nazi Germany saw him employ the largest single airborne lift operation in history.

Germany was struggling to retain its war effort and here, on the east bank of the Rhine River, its defences were already unhinged by the Allied artillery bombardment, the successive cross-river assault of thousands of troops – by the power and might of the attacking Allied army. Expertly deployed thus far, the Allies were about to unleash another huge psychological initiative with a flanking manoeuvre from the Allied airborne divisions.

The two divisions – the British 6th and the American 17th – arrived low and slow; they sought to seize and hold the wooded high ground above Wesel. They flew from airfields in Belgium, France (around Paris) and England to play a part in the second phase of this extremely tough undertaking. Their role, once they were securely inserted into enemy territory, was to secure the main body of their forces against German mobile armour counterattacks. Seizing high ground and bridges over the River Issel was crucial to defending the bridgehead, and for the subsequent breakout from it. This airborne operation, including some 22,000 men, was the largest single-lift, one-day, one-location airborne insertion in history. Operation Varsity, in support of Operation Plunder, saw the airborne divisions go in after, not before, the main attack force. They set off from a point close in to their objectives, only having to travel a few miles forward – and they came with much close-air (fighter aircraft) support. The lessons from Operation Market Garden had been learned.

'Low and slow' was good for the accuracy of the drop – the glider pilots found their landing zones (LZs) and the paratroopers their drop zones (DZs). But 'low and slow' was also good for the accuracy of the heavily concentrated anti-aircraft crews; they excelled at hitting incoming aircraft, downing the gliders and transports, killing those inside them.

The risk was real, the threat was painfully observable – airborne warfare was made brutally visible and cruelly laid bare. A maelstrom of 'ack ack' shell fire from deadly four-barrelled 20mm flak guns tore into the fragile, flimsy wood-and-canvas constructed gliders, ripping apart their fuselages and slamming into the bodies, bones and flesh of those inside. Explosions, fragmentation and disintegration occurred; wings were blown off, entire aircraft were ignited and imploded, and the burning bodies of human beings plunged headlong to the ground in a grotesque and grim slaughter. All told, in excess of one hundred gliders and towing aircraft were brought down and well over three hundred were damaged – among them were those whose landings were far from ideal. It was the enormity of the air armada, the sheer vastness of the air assault – over 1,500 towing aircraft bringing in almost as many gliders, protected by nearly 1,000 fighter aircraft – that guaranteed its successful completion. In all, it took over three hours for the continual airborne insertion of paras and glider-borne troops to be delivered to their drop zones and landing zones.

Pilot Officer Brian Bertram Considine, born in Dublin, January 1920, flew a Dakota towing a glider with 48 Squadron RAF during the Rhine crossing. He had flown a Hurricane with 238 Squadron at Tangmere during the Battle of Britain – one of some forty with Irish connections to have participated. On 21 July 1940, he claimed the destruction of a Messerschmitt 110; a few weeks later, on 27 August 1940, he was involved in the successful interception of a Dornier 17 over Plymouth. He was subsequently shot down himself by a Messerschmitt 109 on 5 November. He bailed out, wounded, but survived. He was to serve in the Middle East, Malta and Sicily, and it was from Cairo that he returned to the UK. After this, he became involved in the

Rhine crossing operation. Considine's family came from Limerick, but at the time of his birth, his father, a doctor, was governor of the Criminal Lunatic Asylum in Dundrum, Dublin. After Operation Varsity, he went to India, carrying out supply drops in Burma. Released from the RAF in December 1945, he flew with Aer Lingus for four years, then went into advertising. He died on 31 March 1996.

The purpose of this mammoth airborne operation was for the troops involved to capture key terrain, bridges and towns in order to assist the surface river-assault troops who were securing a foothold across the Rhine River near the villages of Diersfordt, Schnappenberg and Hamminkeln, and the town of Wesel; they also aimed to clear part of the Diersfordter Wald (Diersfordt Forest) of German forces. The operation was a success, the two airborne divisions holding the seized terrain until the advancing river-crossing units of the 21st Army Group linked up with them, whereupon they joined in the general advance into northern Germany. Lloyd Clark, in his 2008 *Crossing the Rhine*, describes how 'some of the fighting was at extremely close quarters, particularly when gliders crashed into German positions and the infantry carved into the defenders'. The 2nd Battalion Oxfordshire and Buckinghamshire Light Infantry suffered 226 casualties in their systematic clearance of enemy defences and the storming of their objectives. An airborne soldier was a highly specialised fighting man, physically and mentally strong, whose training and tenacity allowed him to operate behind enemy lines, against adversity, with a high level of professionalism and expectation of success. Lightly armed, highly trained and motivated, he is nothing if not adaptable and audacious. Yet there is a word that every airborne soldier dreads; five letters that fill him with foreboding: tanks. Because often he is not properly equipped to counter the threat.

Colonel Jack Carson and his 1st Battalion Royal Ulster Rifles (1/RUR), also known as 'The Rifles', had seized their objective – one of the bridges over the River Issel – having successfully managed to land within fifty yards of it. The Germans, now recovering from the surprise, were launching a series of counterattacks to regain possession of the bridge. It was now up to 1/RUR to hold out against this series of German assaults – a combination of infantry, armoured cars and self-propelled guns. Fighting fiercely and already hard-put to sustain an effective defence of their seized objective, it was then that they heard the fearful five-letter word, 'tanks', being reported. You cannot fight tanks with small arms, rifles, and light (Bren) machine guns. Fortunately, in the event, the tanks were in fact two armoured personnel carriers; rifleman Paddy Devlin let fly into their midst with his Bren gun. He did not cause it to stop, but two six-pounder anti-tank guns positioned to cover the road did. A PIAT (a bazooka-like anti-armour weapon) was deployed to ensure that no further forward movement threatened the bridge.

Close-quarter small unit actions of a similar type were occurring throughout the contested countryside. Sufficiently tenacious, their dogged determination prevented them from being dislodged until the successful link-up with the main river-crossing body occurred. Operation Plunder and Operation Varsity were a success. There to see and report on it – one among a group of members of the press – was Denis Johnston from Ballsbridge, Dublin, a BBC War Correspondent and later the father of Jennifer Johnston, a noteworthy Irish novelist.

The Allies were over the Rhine: Patton at Oppenheim, Bradley at Remagen, and now Montgomery at Wesel. It was time to pursue the retreating Germans once again – to exploit the advantage and to carry the war deeper and deeper into Germany. Significantly, this time the German defeat meant they had neither replacements nor equipment to fill the personnel and capabilities gap; nor did they have space to manoeuvre, territorially. Their lines of communication were severely interrupted, their mobility and freedom of movement critically disrupted. The nature of their defeat was far more decisive and the speed of the Allied rate of advance now exceeded even their own expectations. They were operating in great depth on narrow thrust lines, with armoured spearheads either overrunning enemy areas of resistance or bypassing them, later to attack from the flanks or rear. The Wehrmacht's case was lost, the European war was reaching its last moments, the Nazi regime was facing utter destruction. Their surrender remained elusive; Hitler and the Third Reich were not for capitulation. The war in Europe was not yet over, the fighting would go on. The dying and devastation was not yet at an end.

5

DEVELOPING THE SITUATION

The Rhine crossed, the battle over, the Allies moving further into Germany. The Germans were unyielding and showed no signs of giving up, so the war carried on and the Allies continued to be shot at and shelled. The dying, too, continued. Soldiers had no option but to fight on and try to stay alive.

With the outcome no longer in doubt, the Allies nonetheless remained scared to death; all around them, the human tragedy was relentless. RAF Flight Lieutenant Derek Lugar, Dublin, died in March 1945. Ironically, he was killed in action while bombing the native land of both his German-born grandparents, Anton and Clara Ann Lugar. Anton had come to Ireland as a teacher at King's Hospital; his son, Captain Arthur Lugar, 1st Battalion Leinster Regiment, was killed in August 1918. Amid all the other unjustifiable loss of millions of lives throughout the war, Derek's death, too, was a senseless, irrational, unacceptable waste. He and those he was bombing were caught up in a vortex of violence, a horrible drama of destruction. Ill-prepared to resist the Allies further, the German army was effectively finished. And yet there remained die-hard German troops who fought on ferociously. The merciless cruelty and inhuman viciousness did not end; the wild, untamed, bloodthirsty barbarity was unfinished.

The war was virtually won. The Germans were in total retreat; Hitler was in full denial; the Russians were approaching. How now was Eisenhower to develop the situation? Montgomery wrote in his 1958 memoir:

> War is a political instrument; once it is clear you are going to win,
> political considerations must influence its further course. It became
> obvious to me in the autumn of 1944 that the way things were being
> handled was going to have repercussions far beyond the end of the
> war; it looked to me then as if we were going to 'muck it up'. I reckon
> we did.

Monty felt that the Americans could not understand that it was of little avail
to win the war strategically if it was lost politically. Eisenhower had received
no policy directive from his superiors in Washington, reflecting this British
sense of urgency.

Campaign design, the 'how' of the commander's plan, is the organised
course of action, through a series of military operations, set to achieve the
aim of a given strategic military mission. General Eisenhower, the Allied
Supreme Commander in Europe, was given his mission by the Combined
Chiefs of Staff. It stated, 'You will enter the continent of Europe and, in
conjunction with the United Nations, undertake operations aimed at the
heart of Germany and the destruction of her armed forces.'

The consideration of political objectives can sometimes influence the
planning and direction of military activity in a war. Eisenhower's intention
was to fight and win the war, and his plans for achieving this major goal
remained purely within the military realm. Advancing on a broad front,
from Switzerland to the North Sea, and the Rhine no longer an obstacle,
he would soon have to re-orientate his manoeuvres for the next and final
phase of the campaign in Europe. Montgomery's 21st Army Group was a
strong British/Canadian force with the addition of two American armies,
and it was positioned in the north; Bradley's Twelfth Army Group was
in the centre; General Jacob L. Devers' Sixth Army Group was in the
south. All were progressing eastwards at an unexpected rate of advance.
What rationale would form Eisenhower's 'guidance' to these commanders?
What logic would have his commanders understand his purpose when
interpreting it on the ground? Was he to direct a no-holds-barred race to
Berlin? Was this still relevant to his military mission, as originally tasked,
or had circumstances changed? Was Berlin and its capture central to the
mission's success?

Winston Churchill, Sir Alan Brooke and Montgomery all believed time was of the essence – that, if they were to achieve a post-war political balance in Europe and win a sustainable peace, time was running out. Otherwise the European war, won militarily, might be lost politically. Their chance involved, they thought, Anglo-American forces reaching Berlin, Vienna and Prague – but Berlin, particularly – ahead of the Russians.

Field Marshal Sir Alan Brooke, Chief of the Imperial General Staff (CIGS), was from Colebrook, County Fermanagh, the son of Sir Victor Brooke and Lady Brooke. They were granted land in County Donegal during the Elizabethan era, and, a year after the 1641 rebellion, they were rewarded with more – 30,000 acres in County Fermanagh – for defending what they already had. Brooke was among a number of British generals who had connections with Ireland – be it through birth, upbringing, ancestry, domicile, education or family background – and were involved in the conduct of the war. A formidable figure, he was to prove to be, for the British army, a necessary and effective bulwark against the unwelcome intrusions and interferences of Churchill.

The 'Big Three' – Roosevelt, Stalin and Churchill – had met at Yalta, Crimea, on the Black Sea, on 4 February 1945; Roosevelt, Churchill and the Combined Chiefs of Staff had met in Malta, beforehand, in January. At Yalta, Stalin wanted Allied assistance: to bomb German cities on the axis in order for the Russian army to advance. An agreement was reached on the separation of Germany and Austria into three zones, and a decision made that free elections would be held in the countries overrun by Russia.

The development that would bring these agreements into effect was still at some point in the future. Eisenhower was left to direct military matters on the ground, on the basis of the same unaltered mission as before. Also, some of the old antagonisms, not fully reconciled, surfaced again; the issue of command came to the fore once more, albeit in a different guise. Matters on the ground were going well for the Allies, but behind-the-scenes relationships between them were becoming strained. Churchill and Brooke floated the notion of replacing Air Chief Marshal Sir Arthur Tedder, Deputy Supreme Commander at Supreme Headquarters Allied Expeditionary Force and Eisenhower's second-in-command, with British Field Marshal Harold Alexander, Officer Commanding of the Italian campaign, on the basis that he was an experienced and able ground commander, not an airman, and so was better able to assist Eisenhower with the ongoing land battle. Alexander's family roots went back several centuries in Ireland. Originally Scottish planters, they settled first in County Donegal, then moved to Derry. An ancestor, who amassed wealth in India in the late eighteenth century, built Caledon Castle in County Tyrone, which became the family seat. Thus, Harold Alexander spent his early years at Caledon, with summer holidays in County Donegal. Educated at Harrow, he entered Sandhurst and, in 1911, was commissioned to the Irish Guards.

Perturbed by the implications of this dissatisfaction within command, Eisenhower met with Montgomery and there the matter ended: in the climate of the times, this proposal would have been completely unacceptable among the US generals, the US press, the US public and the US government. That irksome issue taken off the table, next to raise its head was the contentious question of 'narrow thrust' versus 'broad front'; having progressed beyond the Rhine River situation, there was the matter of the best next step. Montgomery advocated strongly for the main effort coming from the Ruhr valley, where he commanded the weight of the Allied advance. Bradley, with the Twelfth Army Group in the centre, was making major advances; to a lesser extent – though it was still impressive – Devers was doing the same in the south. Each wanted the renown of being known as the one who seized Berlin. Montgomery had believed his was the 'main effort', militarily; that it would lead to the capture of Berlin. Eisenhower, however, was becoming less convinced that the taking of Berlin was to be considered a priority objective – seeing it as more of a geographical location than a place of geopolitical significance. With this in mind, he transferred General Simpson's Ninth US Army – one of two 'under command' of Montgomery – and gave it to General Bradley's Twelfth Army Group. Three factors shaped Eisenhower's mindset – and his ideas of how best to develop the situation. Of these influences, one was Russian, one was German, and one was American. All three were military considerations – they were not political. Politics was not his responsibility.

The Russians were closer to Berlin, thirty-eight miles east, on the banks of the Oder River – the Allies were 200 miles to the west of the German capital. However, the far larger brunt of the German army was facing the

Russians. So in a race for Berlin, it was possible that the Allies could reach it first. Montgomery was desperate to make that dash and requested, when writing to Eisenhower, that he be allowed to do so. Eisenhower considered the consequences of entering that contest. There would be a winner and a loser, either the Allies or the Russians. One would be triumphant, the other embarrassed. This, for him, was a consideration. But the far larger concern was the fearful possibility of two armies hurtling themselves headlong at the one objective, from either direction, without any measures in place to avoid a catastrophic collision in the fog of war. There was no preventative control or demarcated limit to the advance of either army – no communication and liaison to avert the likelihood of this risk occurring.

The second great determinant was the possibility of the Germans forming organised resistance areas, particularly in mountainous country in the south, and specifically in the Bavarian Alps. Increasingly, reports of the probable last-stand location of the Nazi regime placed it in that formidable mountainous region of 20,000 square miles; it straddled Bavaria in southern Germany, western Austria and northern Italy, and centred around Berchtesgaden, Hitler's mountaintop hideaway. These mountainous peaks, between 7,000 and 9,000 feet in height, were reinforced with interlocking networks of fortified strong points and defensive positions; these positions concealed anti-aircraft defences and secret installations with already-stockpiled munitions, poison gas supplies and even Messerschmitt jet fighter production facilities.

There was a formidable mountain defence system in an area referred to as Alpenfestung ('the Alpine Fortress'). The almost impregnable topography, together with the reported existence of these massive concrete bomb-proof bunkers, could prove to be an enormous and frightening impediment to the end of the European war. Hitler and the Third Reich could continue their bitter fight for years from this alarming Alpine superstructure, making use of 'Werewolf', a supposedly specially trained commando-type resistance force. Such defensive ambitions were consistent with what the Allies were already experiencing – the Germans had adapted a 'fight and stand' form of resistance wherever they could posture; it was a fanatical refusal to surrender despite the fact that it was the only militarily rational thing to do.

Thirdly, and perhaps most significantly, a carefully worded cable sent by General George C. Marshall, US Chief of Staff and Eisenhower's superior officer and mentor, addressed the twin problems facing Eisenhower – a Russian advance and German defence – and made subtle suggestions for his consideration, outlining possible courses of action.

With these considerations, Eisenhower weighed up the possibility of an unintended slaughterhouse clash with the Russians over a city now without significance, as it was unlikely to host Hitler and his regime; they were likely to make a break to establish themselves in the Alpenfestung of southern Germany. Eisenhower's job, as he saw it, was to have the war over quickly and to see the German army destroyed as fast as possible. Thus, he was decided on how he would develop the situation at this crucial turning point of the war. Only, of course, matters were not solely up to him. Hitler and his SS henchmen from the Third Reich had a say, and they were determined to fight on regardless in the name of honour, the Fatherland, and the delusional belief that victory was somehow still possible.

From a position of one-time supreme strength, the Wehrmacht were now depleted and struggling, their exhausted forces suffering. Hitler, however, was indifferent to their condition; he had neither interest nor sympathy for their plight, and was unconcerned about their predicament.

Hundreds of thousands of Germans were killed fighting for the Nazi regime long after defeat was inevitable. Hitler, aware of the mounting military collapse, was nonetheless impervious to the scale of the unfolding human tragedy. He blamed his defeats on the battle-hardened generals whom he regarded as having betrayed him. He dismissed their valid suggestions as unacceptable criticism. Instead, he surrounded himself with odious, servile staff – generals Keital, Jodel, Krebs, Doenitz, Himmler, Goebbels and Goering – who supported him and remained unquestioningly loyal despite his fanatical refusal to surrender. Hitler's huge vanity and his obedient military now became a primary hazard; instead of protecting Germany's own people, they condemned them to useless sacrifice.

The 'Master Race' was now without a master plan. Fantasy and fanaticism was substituted for strategy. Hitler's strict insistence on fixed defences, fortress cities, maniac militancy, and the uses of Goebbels' 'wonder weapons' propaganda blinded them to the reality that the fortunes of war, as they now stood, were irreversible. Hitler and the hardliners, with much of Berlin already reduced to rubble by frequent Allied bombing raids, were committed to a fight to the death.

German losses were staggering but Hitler held to the calamitous illusion that the coalition of the Allied powers and the Soviet Union could yet split apart, and that the scope for negotiation may yet lead to a circumstance where some semblance of a settlement was salvageable. Defeat in the Ardennes put an end to this possibility and yet negotiating from a position of weakness was not something the narcissistic Hitler was prepared to do. So the German army were forced to fight to the very end and the German people were brought to the point of total destruction. Hitler's plans were a continuation of the same lost cause, bringing the country and its people into the abyss.

In the closing months of the Second World War, Nazi Germany saw the instigation of the Volksstrum ('people's storm'), a home guard, made up of any able-bodied 'men', ranging from 16 year old boys to elderly men of 60. Often, however, the boys were between 12 and 15 years old, and the elderly 65 and above. They were with Panzerfaust, a personally fired anti-tank weapon, and a machine gun; they were easy to use, plentiful and munitions for them were available. Inculcated with the incredulous belief that final victory was still possible, the Volksstrum's main objective was to assist in halting the advance of the Allied and Soviet Red Army forces. Propagandised as a force that would turn the tide in the war effort, it could only ever be an ineffective and unreliable force – its net effect was only to see more sent out to die. But the Allies were also dying, the Irish among them.

Brigadier General William Anthony Sheil, from Dublin, originally in the Royal Artillery, became a staff officer with the 51st Division, and, from June 1944, went all the way through France, the Netherlands and Belgium, into Germany. Returning to HQ after attending a conference in Reesum, a village east of Breman, he changed places with his driver who had become tired. The jeep subsequently went over a mine and he was killed. His driver, in the passenger seat, fortunately escaped with minor injuries. This happened nine days before the end of the war in Europe, on 29 April 1945 (VE Day took place on 8 May). Brigadier Sheil is buried in the Reichswald War Cemetery. Having joined the army first in 1915, he served in France towards the close of the First World War, after which he had become adjutant of the Army School of Equitation, retiring in 1935. Rejoining in 1939, he was in command of the 10th Field Regiment Royal Artillery in France in 1940 and was evacuated from Dunkirk. He then trained with the 128th Field Regiment, 51st Highland Infantry Division in El Alamein, where he was awarded his first Distinguished Service Order (DSO); he was awarded the bar to his DSO in Sicily. He briefly returned to Britain before re-entering France with the division in June 1944, fighting throughout Northwestern Europe until the war's end neared. Throughout a life spent in service, he endured the sacrifices, hardships and jeopardy which that war generation experienced.

Sheil had fallen in a war that ought not to have persisted beyond the Allies' breaching of the Rhine, once the outcome became inevitable. It was now impossible to force an outcome other than defeat, but Hitler was beyond rational. Instead, a tremendous cost in human lives was exchanged for the furtherance of the Third Reich. It was a death sentence for the German people. Hitler considered that the best people had already fallen; if the war was lost, it was immaterial to him if the people perished too. Many people, not only Germans, were to die in vain before the war ended – before the war was made to finally end. His 'fighting' generals were all too aware of the predicament: it was their troops who were facing impossible odds and perishing. Few were brave enough to confront Hitler with the facts as they were. Heinz Guderian and Gotthard Heinrici, both colonel generals, were among the exceptions, informing Hitler of the non-existent armies and divisions that he deludedly continued to believe remained fully intact, up to strength and equipped. Hitler and his staff spoke of 'reserves', which were either not there or amounted to untrained, inexperienced, unequipped replacements that were not in any way equal to the task. Dared to be informed that these were inadequate – disabused of his version of 'reality' – Hitler would erupt into volcanic rages of uncontrollable temper, yelling incoherently with outbursts of empty phrases or irrational diatribes: tirades exclaiming that life never forgives weaknesses and to have faith in the Fatherland and belief in success. This was neither solution nor salvation. The fighting would continue until Hitler finally lost all belief in a favourable outcome, but of course by then many had died needlessly.

Before that, still navigating the likelihood of dealing with the Russians after the war, Churchill was very unhappy with Eisenhower's 'new' direction. As far as he was concerned, he was determined that the Allies should take Berlin and, in light of this, it was 'highly important that we should shake hands with the Russians as far to the east as possible'. Marshall and Eisenhower maintained their focus on the mission on the ground, and so it was from there that the situation was developed. Field Marshal Montgomery's 21st Army Group (minus the 9th US Army) was tasked with the urgent initiative of seizing the German ports in the north to end the U-boat war. The plan was also, crucially, to head off the Russians from getting into Schleswig-Holstein and then occupying Denmark, thus controlling the entrance to the Baltic. Lastly, it would open up communications with Sweden again, making available heretofore idle Norwegian and Swedish shipping.

In the centre, Bradley's Twelfth Army would advance on a line that passed through Erfurt, Leipzig and Dresden (the last, 100 miles south of Berlin) to split the German army in two. Devers' Sixth Army Group, in the south, headed to cut off access to the Alpenfestung, which Eisenhower called 'the mountain citadel', in the Bavarian Alps. Tasked accordingly, the commanders went to fight their last battles – their goal was to ensure Hitler and the Third Reich that their cause was lost. The stage was set: the German war was reaching its last moments.

6

FIGHTING ON ANOTHER FRONT

The aerial chase was ongoing for some time. The Messerschmitt 109 fighter aircraft was like glue stuck to the tail of Casey's Bristol Blenheim light bomber. In and out of cloudbanks they flew, going high, suddenly diving low, twisting, turning, banking sharply, skilfully skipping over countryside contours, barely skimming over hilltops, hedge hopping, tree topping, only feet above roofs. Flight Lieutenant Michael James O'Brien Casey, known as 'Mike', was giving it total throttle, manoeuvring madly using adroit aerobatics. Mike Casey and his crew of two, an observer and wireless operator/air gunner from 54 (Blenheim) Squadron, were flying a reconnaissance mission over the Wesel–Bocholt area of Germany when they were spotted by Lieutenant Hans-Folkert Rosenboom. That he was unable to get a satisfactory 'fix' or line of fire on Casey's Blenheim was due to the operational flying skills of the young Irishman – Casey was indeed leading him on a merry chase.

Michael Casey's father, Michael Lewis Casey, had an address at Hollywood, County Kildare, and he was the Inspector General of the Indian Police Service in Allahabad, northern India, where Mike was born on 19 February 1918. Mike Casey attended Clongowes Wood College when he was nine years old and continued there for three years, afterwards going to Stonyhurst College boarding school in England. Popular and a good sportsman, he displayed prowess in boxing, cricket and rugby; these qualities as a competitor, fighter and team player were to hold him in good stead as a pilot with the RAF.

The aerial chase with Rosenboom was 16 October 1939. The war was not long started, but in this instance it was very much in full swing. Mike Casey was using every evasive manoeuvre recommended, his instinctive handling of the aircraft and its instantaneous response helping him and his crew stay alive as the Messerschmitt cannon shells tore past them. Mike might momentarily succeed in shaking Rosenboom off his tail, but he was just as quickly on him again. He was conscious not to maintain level flight, using ploys and tactics to outrun the Messerschmitt, but the mismatch in their respective aircrafts' manoeuvrability eventually presented itself, even if for a split second or two. Nevertheless, it was enough, and the Messerschmitt's cannons found their mark this time, seriously damaging the Blenheim. Already scarcely head height above the surface of the ground, Casey had no time to lower the undercarriage and yet managed to safely land it in an open field. They managed to scramble free of the aircraft not a moment too soon, as the Blenheim exploded in a huge fireball. Nonetheless, defiantly, they gave Hans-Folkert Rosenboom a recalcitrant wave as he circled overhead – as much as to say 'you got our aircraft but you did not get us'. Downed well behind enemy lines, it was not long before they were captured by the Germans and Casey was sent to Stalag Luft I near Barth.

For a captured soldier, airman or sailor, the fighting may be over, but the war is not and the struggle goes on. To escape is the front they now fight on, and such matters are not conducted without patience and purpose. With this in mind, 'escape committees' are formed and matters are co-ordinated to ensure efforts are synchronised and under collaborative control. This ensures that the escape attempt with the best possibility of succeeding is the one that receives the best support and that other exertions do not jeopardise efficiency and the outcome of the main escape attempt.

There are other ways to fight, and one of them was to hide: to become a ghost within the POW camp and unaccounted for in roll calls. Such actions would lead the Germans into thinking you, and others like you, had escaped. This would force them to undertake extended, thorough, frustrating, confusing searches, tying up their resources in attempts to look for escapees that could not be found – escapees that had not, in fact, escaped in the first place.

Mike Casey was one such 'bad boy' among a group of inmates who went missing. For his efforts as an escapee in 1942, he was sent to the black, grim, isolated, reputedly escape-proof Stalag Luft III – the main camp for airmen – in Lower Silesia, close to the town of Sagan (now Zagan) taken over in the Polish invasion. Notwithstanding its reputation, an escape commitment was formulated and actively pursued. Mike Casey was part of the escape committee; he was 'strong box' treasurer and concealment officer, in charge of the safe keeping and concealment of all forged documents, papers and money.

Stalag Luft III was opened in May 1942. The site was selected because it was remote and considered to pose a considerable hindrance to inmates who might contemplate tunnelling an escape. It was eventually to house 11,000 aircrew prisoners. The majority were American, but there was a sizeable minority of about 2,500 British prisoners, and about a thousand airmen of mixed nationalities. From mid-1943, a newly built north compound was completed. It was protected by 100 guards from the original camp, and housed the majority of the British aircrew. It was from here that the men of the escape committee seriously put their minds to work about how best to effect an escape. They knew they were very far east and in a remote location, adding considerably to the difficulty of getting all the way safely back to Britain. They knew the chances of success were slim, but if any escape attempt were to cause disruption to the Germans, this in itself was considered worthy of their efforts – as it would be part of the overall war effort.

In the event, the escape committee, having considered a suggested escape option to be a worthwhile undertaking, also decided that they would go big and try and get as many men out as possible – 200 of them, all at the one time. It was to be the single greatest escape attempt ever undertaken by Allied POWs during the Second World War. It was later portrayed in the Hollywood blockbuster *The Great Escape*, starring Steve McQueen, Richard Attenborough and James Garner. The movie was a fictionalised version rather than a rigorously historic account, cinematic and commercial considerations winning out.

The actual escape plan envisaged the digging of three tunnels, codenamed Tom, Dick and Harry. Tunnelling, and not being discovered in the process, presents a whole litany of challenges. Digging underground for any distance requires implements for burrowing underground, soil extraction, removal and concealment; wood to shore up the weight of the overhead earth, preventing collapse; and light to dig by. This is not to mention the physical and mental challenge – a group of workers had to be able to work in claustrophobic conditions and cope with the constant fear of cave-in and suffocation, or discovery by the camp guards and whatever the consequences might be there. Preparations also required the forging of documents that could withstand close and careful scrutiny, attire that would not attract attention or suspicion, and money. The considerations involved in any escape attempt were many and complex. 'Tom' was discovered not long after it was commenced, so it was considered prudent to concentrate on the continued construction of 'Harry' only, using what space existed in 'Dick' to deposit and conceal the removed soil. Hut 104 was the tunnel entry point and its finished length was 350 feet into a wooded area beyond the furthest exterior fence. The night of 24 March 1944 was chosen for the escape; the important decision that remained was the selection of the 200 men that would effect the escape. Sensibly, priority was given to those who were considered to have the best chance: German speakers had better preference, and so on. The remaining places were decided by a lottery draw, the random chance of a raffle. This was how their fates were decided – who had a bid for freedom or who stayed in captivity. Both circumstances had an uncertain future.

As it happened, this chance action of escape was discovered before all 200 men got out. Nonetheless, seventy-six men did manage to get beyond the tunnel. 'Harry' had done its job. Now, in small groups, pairs, or as individuals, the fugitive escapees made their attempts at fleeing westwards. Only three ultimately made it back safely to Britain – two Norwegian and one Dutch aircrew. Through mishaps, unlucky setbacks, misadventure, perhaps inevitable happenstance, the rest were captured. Such was the extent of the manhunt undertaken on the orders of a furious Hitler. He was so infuriated that he had instructed that all recaptured escapees be shot. In the end, fifty of them were – Mike Casey among them. Casey had headed south in the company of one other escapee; they were in the guise of foreign war workers. When stopped by police near Gorlitz, their fake papers did not stand up to close scrutiny; they were immediately arrested and brought to the town jail, where they met up with four other recaptured escapees. On 31 March 1944, all six were taken to a nearby wood and, under the direction of a Gestapo agent, shot dead by accompanying troops. Their remains were ordered to be cremated at Gorlitz.

The remains of 'the fifty' – the escapees shot by the Gestapo – along with all other RAF aircrew that were shot down and believed dead or missing, were subsequently searched for by the RAF MRES. The MRES was able to account for over two-thirds of the missing personnel, and among them was the aforementioned Fred O'Donovan, who considered his work there 'the best, most fulfilling and honourable thing I did in my entire life'.

Coincidentally, Fred's brother Sean, also in the British army, had a notorious history as an escape artist. Sean took his father's bike in Dublin and cycled all the way to Belfast and joined the Royal Artillery. Shortly after training, he was to find himself posted to North Africa. As a forward observation officer (responsible for calling in artillery fire and 'fall of shot' corrections) in late October 1942, he accompanied a group of commandos around the El Alamein area. Their missions involved night raids – infiltrations behind German lines, destroying Axis fuel dumps and thus weakening German mobility. After one such raid, a navigation error saw them captured by the Germans, whose strict stance concerning British commandos was that they were to be shot. After receiving 'rough treatment', matters were looking bleak; only chance intervened when a German 'senior officer' wished to inspect the commando prisoners. It was none other than the Desert Fox, Erwin Rommel himself. Sean O'Donovan spoke up, telling Rommel of the treatment they had received, and that they were going to be shot. Impressed by his impertinence, Rommel rewarded him by granting the group a reprieve from death. This, however, involved imprisonment in Tobruk, North Africa.

Within two weeks, Sean and two colleagues escaped imprisonment, only to fall foul of the immensity of the desert and be recaptured. They were handed over to the Italian army and transferred to Reggio in Italy via Palermo in Sicily. Sean escaped once again and joined the Italian partisans (the resistance) in Calabria, fighting alongside them for a hugely exciting nine months. Informed upon, he was once again captured and faced death a second time. Using some Irish blarney, he managed to convince the prison camp's English-speaking chaplain, who had learned his English from Irish priests in Rome, to persuade the Italian camp commandant to give him a

71

reprieve. He was granted this reprieve but was again transferred – this time to the Luckenwalde POW camp in Germany.

For some reason, the Germans placed all the 'Irish by birth, Irish by extraction, Irish by choice and Irish by chance' in the one POW camp. Among other distinctions, the 'O' in one's surname was used to identify one's nationality; a mixed grouping resulted, including some from America and even one from Sierra Leone. With a number of escape attempts foiled at an early stage, it dawned on the inmates that there must be a German plant, or plants, among them, so those that could resorted to speaking Irish among themselves. The Germans responded with a 'get tough' regime: there were food restrictions, Red Cross food parcels failed to appear, and conditions generally deteriorated within the camp. Orders were issued that meant letters to next-of-kin, which were allowed under the Geneva Convention, would not pass the camp's censor unless they were written in English.

It was about this time that a letter arrived in Dublin, written in English, that described conditions in Luckenwalde POW camp as being quite acceptable. The letter ended quite innocently with the words, 'Give my love to Moryha.' Since no such lady existed, it was not too difficult to translate 'Moryha' into the Gaelic '*mar dheadh*'; from this it was apparent that the letter contained a deliberate tissue of lies. As a result, immediate representations were made to the International Red Cross in Geneva and, in due course, a delegation from Switzerland arrived in Luckenwalde to investigate. Naturally, by the time they arrived, conditions had improved beyond belief, and all as a result of a simple Irish word. Sean O'Donovan escaped from Luckenwalde not long afterwards, but was soon recaptured. In order to teach him a lesson, he was stripped of his clothing, put in a goods wagon, and sent by train to Neuruppin work camp near Berlin. The German capital, in April 1945, was being bombed regularly – the RAF by night and the USAF by day. Sean and other inmates were organised into work parties to clear the resultant rubble, debris, fragments of stone, brick and other masonry off the roads. They were not permitted to enter the air raid shelters during bombing raids, so it was very dangerous work. Being marched along a road one day, Sean approached a route that was choked with a retreating German army and fleeing refugees; at this point, two Russian fighter aircraft strafed the scene. Sean seized a German military map from an overturned vehicle and noticed it was of the local area; he took advantage of the confusion and pandemonium going on around him and decided to make a break for it – he walked away unnoticed.

Another opportunist escape attempt was successfully undertaken by Cork-born Major Mervyn Dennison, A Company, 3rd Parachute Battalion. He was involved in the action at Arnhem, and for his conduct during the battle he was awarded the Military Cross, with the following passage coming from the citation for his award:

> Major Dennison commanded A Company of the 3rd Parachute Battalion which had been dropped West of Arnhem on 17 September 1944. During the advance on the town on the evening of 17 September the battalion was held up and shortly afterwards Major Dennison's company in the rear came under small arms and heavy mortar fire from the flank. Major Dennison led two platoons of his company and overran three enemy machine gun posts which formed the nucleus of the opposition on the flank. On the following morning Major Dennison's Company acted as a rear guard to the Battalion advance on Arnhem, but was cut off from the remainder of the battalion by strong enemy forces. Later the Battalion got into serious difficulties and Major Dennison, with reserve ammunition, was ordered to fight his way through at all costs. This he did successfully against very strong opposition. Throughout both these actions Major Dennison showed a high standard of personal courage, leadership and determination. Even when severely wounded in both arms, he continued to encourage and inspire his men.

Major Mervyn Dennison was wounded while struggling with a German infantryman; the German was trying to run him through with his bayonet and Dennison used his hands to defend himself during the fight. He found himself in this predicament just after having regained consciousness following a mortar shell that exploded close to him. Another member of A Company, realising the danger, came to his assistance and quickly despatched the attacking German. At battle's end, Dennison was placed among the wounded, taken prisoner and moved to Germany. He was taken to Oflag IX, a POW camp located in a castle. With the Russians advancing, the camp was closed and the inmates were marched westwards under close supervision of guards along with guard dogs. Taking advantage of their circumstance, other prisoners blew cigarette smoke at the guard dogs' eyes, temporarily blinding them – under cover of this distraction, Dennison and a lieutenant slipped away. They successfully made their way to American lines and were repatriated to England.

Major General Adrian Carton de Wiart VC was also incarcerated in a castle, Vincigliata Castle outside Florence. Half-Irish, half-Belgian, and 62 years of age, Carton de Wiart was a veteran of the First World War and others, going back to the Boer War; he had over a dozen wounds, was missing his left hand, and had a black eyepatch. His mother was Irish; his father was a Belgian lawyer and of an aristocratic background. Nicknamed the 'Unkillable Soldier', Carton de Wiart looked as though his end had finally come when both engines on the aircraft in which he was travelling cut out and the pilot had to ditch it into the sea, a mile off the coast of Italy. The impact with the sea's surface knocked him temporarily unconscious, but on coming to he managed to successfully swim to shore, where he was taken prisoner by the Italians and sent to the huge medieval castle in Tuscany.

There, Carton de Wiart met Richard O'Connor, a like-minded daredevil. General Richard ('Dick') O'Connor was also half-Irish: the O'Connor family was from Ballybrack in County Offaly. Major Maurice O'Connor was serving in India, with Princess Victoria's Royal Irish Fusiliers, when Richard was born in Srinagar, Kashmir, in August 1889. Maurice O'Connor sustained injuries in an accident and retired in 1894, returning to Ireland. On his death, the family moved to Scotland, to his mother's home – Lillian Morris, daughter of Sir John Morris. Richard was educated at Wellington College, subsequently entered Sandhurst, and was commissioned into the Cameronians (Scottish Rifles) regiment. He commanded the Western Desert Force in the early years of the Second World War, but was captured by the Germans in 1941 and spent two years in an Italian POW camp. He escaped in 1943 and, in 1944, commanded the VIII Corps, both in the Battle of Normandy and later during Operation Market Garden.

Vincigliata Castle was known as 'Italy's Colditz', after Schloss Colditz Castle in Saxony, Germany. The German camp was converted for use as a POW camp during the Second World War, housing incorrigible, high-risk, repeat Allied escapees. Situated on a rocky outcrop overlooking the

River Mulde, from May 1943 it housed British and American officers. Despite the camp's reputation as escape-proof, various escape attempts were undertaken, some of them successful. Now, in Italy, Carton de Wiart and O'Connor wanted to prove that Vincigliata Castle was no less escape proof. They were utterly determined and succeeded in escaping via a tunnel which took much effort and a long time (seven months) to construct. They had undertaken attempts previously, which were unsuccessful: scaling the walls with improvised ropes, creating carefully concealed holes in the walls, even exploring the possibility of a deep medieval well – but none of these granted freedom. So they decided on the 'hard' option: literally burrowing sixty feet through solid bedrock and making their way cross-country for the Swiss border. County Kerry's Monsignor Hugh O'Flaherty, known as 'the Scarlet Pimpernel of the Vatican', was a visitor to the camp; he smuggled out secret letters for them through which they maintained contact with London. It was, however, to take a third attempt before they managed to effect full freedom, escaping through the tunnel and returning to participate once again in the war effort.

Michael Casey, Sean O'Donovan, Mervyn Dennison, Adrian Carton de Wiart and Richard O'Connor were determined to maintain the fight on another front through great risk – difficult, dangerous and sometimes deadly gambles in which they sought to outwit their captors. For their captors, there was no escaping the inevitable encirclement of the Allies in the west and the Russians in the east. The Germans had become prisoners of their own misdeeds, and the full and horrible extent of this entrapment was about to be graphically revealed.

7

AN INDESCRIBABLE SHOCK

The Second World War had, all along, been about confronting the unexpected. Discovering the concentration camps was about confronting the unimaginable. Their discovery was deeply disturbing to the world as a whole, but for those eyewitnesses who first encountered them, it was incomprehensible to understand how human beings could descend to such depraved depths of evil. Transfixed, stupefied, astonished, they were at a complete loss to comprehend the level of barbarity before them; the magnitude of the horror and the scale of the abominably dire and shocking scenes were beyond understanding. Such deplorable depravity was not supposed to exist in the minds of mankind, yet here, in front of their very eyes, was the all-too-evident proof that it could – and did. The dead, the dying and the dazed were everywhere. Dehydrated, malnourished, skeletal, there were live human carcasses stumbling aimlessly about. They were stumbling past bodies – hundreds and hundreds of bodies. Bodies heaped in piles, decomposing, scattered about individually or in groups, their forms grotesque, their dignity distorted, their dying abhorrent. Searing into the senses, along with the hideous sights, was the pervasive stench of death: the prevalent, extensive, foul smell of the decay of rotting corpses. The rancid, putrid, omnipresent, odious stink of dead humans and human waste. Even in the midst of a brutally fought total war, soldiers were not supposed to witness such total horror – nor were people to perpetrate or suffer it. Ache, agony and anguish; suffering and sorrow. There, among it all, were some small movements of those still dying. Death had them in its grip and was only waiting for them to succumb. Some realised it, others did not.

Rumours and reports of such places and happenings were mostly dismissed as hearsay at the time, or disbelieved as propaganda. But now, in plain sight, the demons were visible on the surface. Many of the survivors in the liberated camps were already some so disease-ridden or weakened by lack of food that they died following liberation. Because of their prolonged starvation, their stomachs and bodies simply could not accept normal food.

Deliberately killed in the gas chambers or by disease or starvation, millions died in death camps first discovered by the Russians as they advanced west across Poland – camps at Majdanek, Treblinka, Birkenau, Chelmno, Belzec and Sobibor. As well as extermination camps, there were work camps like Auschwitz; they were part of an organised system of slave labour, which became a profitable enterprise for the SS. The SS hired out prisoners to factory owners or sent them into armaments and munitions factories and worked them there until they died. The vast scale of resources devoted to this mass murder, even when Germany was facing its final days, was to amaze the Allies as they, too, discovered such camps during their advance eastwards.

On 11 April 1945, American forces liberated the camps at Buchenwald near Weimar and the V-2 rocket-manufacturing slave labour camp at Nordhausen in the Harz Mountains. Irishman Denis Johnston (1901–1984), a BBC war correspondent between 1942 and 1945, was among the first to reach these camps after the retreat of the Germans. He broadcasted a report of what he witnessed and later published an extract from his diary of the war on his experience at Buchenwald; the extract was printed in *The Bell* in March 1951. Arriving just ahead of him was Michael Mulry, from Caltra, County Galway. His sister, Mary Morris of the Queen Alexandra Imperial Military Nursing Service Reserves, wrote a diary of her experiences, now held in the Imperial War Museum – it was the basis for a book edited by Carol Acton, *A Very Private Diary: A Nurse in Wartime*.

Four days after the US troops discovered Buchenwald, British troops liberated Bergen-Belsen, forty-five miles south of Hamburg in Lüneberg Heath. Dubliner David Baynham, on completion of his second year of studying engineering at Trinity College Dublin, joined the Royal Engineers and was posted to 27 Airfield Construction Group. Their aim was to build airstrips as far forward as they possibly could so that RAF bombers (along with fighter escorts) could stay in the air over enemy territory for longer and avail of quick refuelling. Airfield constructions were engaged in all across France, Holland and Germany. Proceeding into northern Germany, Baynham was suddenly informed that he had to hand over virtually all of his earth-moving equipment; he and the other men in his unit were sent to a medical depot to receive injections. They were sent to cut enormous trenches in the ground in order to bury the bodies from Bergen-Belsen concentration camp. Dysentery, tuberculosis and typhus were in danger of further raging out of control and affecting the liberating troops themselves, so the thousands of emaciated naked corpses lying unburied on the open ground, or in the camp hutments, had to be disposed of quickly. In an interview for the NUI Cork Volunteers Project, Baynham disclosed that 'I drove around the perimeter of the camp and looked down into Belsen; there were still [some bodies] lying in open ground, while others were still being rescued. On the main road outside there was the Red Cross and a mobile operating theatre.'

One of those rendering Red Cross care was another Dubliner and a qualified paediatrician, Dr Bob Collis. He had played rugby for Ireland and had worked in the Rotunda in Dublin, Johns Hopkins in Baltimore, USA, and Great Ormond Street in London. He joined the International Red Cross in 1945, finding a desperate need for his expertise there and taking charge of a makeshift children's hospital. Of the concentration camp, he thought, 'The inmates of the camp had been starved during the last winter and now their malnutrition was accentuated by an epidemic of typhus carried by lice and every form of enteritis including typhoid fever was rife. They had been dying at a rate of a thousand a day when the camp was opened by the British army.'

After medical care, those who managed to survive began to recover and were eventually repatriated. There were five orphaned children among the survivors for whom neither home nor family could be found. Collis and a Dutch nurse, Han Hogerzeil, with whom he had begun an affair in Belsen, took responsibility for them and eventually, in late 1946, he took them to Ireland, where Jewish families were found for three of them. The other two, a brother and sister, Zoltan and Edit Zinn from Slovakia, went to live with him, his wife and two sons. When his own children had grown up, Collis divorced his wife Phyllis and married Han, with whom he had a son, Sean. Sean died tragically when he was killed in an accident at the age of thirteen in Nigeria, where Collis had become head of the Institute of Child Health. His 1975 biography, *To Be a Pilgrim*, tells us the full story.

Dubliner Phil Farrington was also among the British troops who helped liberate Bergen-Belsen concentration camp – as was another Dubliner, John Joseph Deegan. Both had taken part in the Normandy landings on D-Day – Deegan arriving on Sword Beach. Deegan was determined on military involvement, maybe even a career, as he sought danger, adventure and excitement. Not having succeeded in joining the Irish Defence Forces at first, because he was a skinny youth, he instead managed to join the British RAF and became part of a unit, the 405 Repair and Salvage Unit, whose task it was to quickly identify the whereabouts of downed Allied aircraft so that they might be repaired or salvaged. To carry out his duty in locating downed aircraft in the field, he had to master a powerful Harley-Davidson motorbike. The bike granted him a certain freedom of movement and made his experience of war all the more personal and singular, as he advanced eastwards from Normandy, through Europe, on to the Battle of the Bulge and into Germany. This was an exhilarating engagement for a then unsophisticated, callow youngster, which dramatically lost all of its appeal when he, too, came upon the concentration camps. His immaturity and naivety, his guileless innocence, suddenly ended with the awful and harrowingly gruesome scenes he was now confronted with. These sights were to change his attitude to life, challenging him deeply. But they also affirmed a belief within him that what the Allies were doing in defying Hitler and the Germans was right – to fight against the Third Reich was to be fighting against evil itself. Only he had not expected this evil to be made manifest so horrendously explicit and vile, 'When we went to Germany, we found it was a worthwhile cause.'

Deegan was among many who were unprepared to witness the unscrupulous and deliberate extermination of the Jews and other minorities. The sheer extent of the calculated, carefully resourced, unearthly and programmatic killing of humans – six million of them – was unfathomable. The six death camp sites in Poland accounted for half of these deaths alone;

they contained gas chambers and large crematoria to facilitate and conduct the 'Final Solution to the Jewish Question'. It took forty years before Deegan – later Brother Columbanus Deegan, a Franciscan friar – spoke of such events publicly, 'That was it for me; I knew there was no glamour in war.' He could not forget what he has witnessed at Belsen. 'I could not shake off the smell of death I experienced that day. I sometimes get flashbacks and the smell returns as if it was yesterday.' British troops present at Belsen were sometimes to recall, after the war, as veterans, an overwhelming amalgam: a loathsome sickly-sweet stink of rotting human flesh and the revoltingly poignant smell of human faeces. It was so strong it could be detected miles outside the camp's perimeter.

The sights, the smells, the reality and the inhumanity were overpowering, causing General Dwight D. Eisenhower to say of similar scenes elsewhere, 'I have never felt able to describe my emotional reactions when I first came face to face with indisputable evidence of Nazi brutality and ruthless disregard of every shred of decency ... I have never at any other time experienced an equal sense of shock.'

With the tide of the war turning, and the pressure of the Russians advancing westwards and the Allies advancing eastwards, the entire camp system began to collapse. As the German army had begun to retreat inwards during the last months of the war, the various camp occupants were marched or transported by train to camps in Germany and Austria. In mid-January 1945, nearly 70,000 prisoners from Auschwitz-Birkenau and its sub-camps were evacuated and made to march westwards in freezing cold weather. Some were somewhat luckier; they were transported in open-top or closed, but heavily overcrowded, railway freight wagons. These marches took weeks to complete and involved appalling conditions, and so on the way to their alternate destinations many died, or, if unable to keep up, were killed. Some 15,000 perished en route to the new camps at Buchenwald, Dachau, Gross-Rosen and Mauthausen (in Austria). Other camps were hastily evacuated in like manner, and on these so-called death marches, a quarter of a million people perished. For those who survived, their arrival into already occupied concentration camps led to overcrowding and, in already poor conditions where the Germans could no longer house or feed the prisoners, widespread starvation and disease resulted and the unburied corpses began to pile up in their thousands. The diseased and dying wandered about, if they were able, in grossly unsanitary and unhygienic conditions. Many weakened survivors, in addition to having chronic physical health difficulties, were suffering from severe psychological problems caused by their horrendous treatment at the hands of their jailers. The concentration camps' liberators, Russian and Allied soldiers, were unprepared for what they found, but immediately tried to help the survivors.

Unprepared, too, were some thirty-two merchant seamen from Ireland sent to work in an SS slave labour camp: punishment for their refusal to voluntarily join the German war effort when they were captured. The camp was located in Farge, northern Germany, where they were tasked to build the Valentin Bunker, the biggest construction site in Germany, employing up to 12,000 slave workers in two twelve-hour shifts. It is believed that around 5,000 slave workers died while constructing the bunker. The Valentin Bunker was specially designed for the construction of a new, revolutionary type of submarine, the XVI U-boat, one of Hitler's 'wonder weapons' or 'miracle boat', with which the Third Reich hoped to achieve the extraordinary phenomenon of even yet snatching victory from defeat. They made strenuous efforts, ruthlessly exploiting prisoners' lives, to produce a new U-boat that would offer the prospect of the Kriegsmarine regaining the upper hand in the Atlantic. David Blake Knox's 2017 book *Hitler's Irish Slaves* gives an insightful account of the Irish involvement in this slave workforce used to construct this immense bunker.

In another astonishing aspect of the war, there were five Irishmen among a group of 160 prisoners whom Himmler and other SS leaders attempted to use in a barter to save the regime, or, as a final resort, themselves, in the final days of the Third Reich. The prisoners included eminent international statesmen, aristocrats and clergy, along with those who opposed German generals and relatives of those who had plotted against Hitler, among them the family of Claus von Stauffenberg, who placed the bomb in Hitler's Wolf's Lair in July 1944.

The hostages included a number of RAF officers, survivors of the famous 'Great Escape', and Colonel John McGrath from Roscommon, a First World War veteran who had left his job as manager of Dublin's Theatre Royal to rejoin the British army in 1939. They had been held with Russian, Italian and Polish special prisoners known as Nacht und Nebel ('Night and Fog') prisoners, whose existence was a state secret. Although generally treated more favourably than regular concentration camp prisoners, they lived in constant danger of execution, a fate some did not escape – including Stalin's son, who died following a fracas with some Irish prisoners. This group of 160 prominent Nazi SS hostages was transported from various concentration camps to the remote Alpine Puster Valley municipality of Niederdorf, located in the east of South Tyrol, close to the Austrian border, in the final days of the Third Reich. The group were known as the 'Prominenten', although not all of them were famous or well known. They were assembled from concentration and POW camps as the 'Thousand Year Reich' collapsed into chaos, ruination and rubble. There were those in the Third Reich – Heinrich Himmler, Ernst Kaltenbrunner and Walter Schellenburg – who made efforts to be the ones to engage the Western Allies in dialogue, removing these prisoners to the Alpine redoubt to prevent their liberation by advancing forces.

Colonel Michael Joseph 'John' McGrath was born in Elphin, County Roscommon. Fighting in the First World War, in Gallipoli and France, he was twice wounded and, as a result of his latter wounds, he was shipped back to England and remained hospitalised for a lengthy period. He survived the war and afterwards was demobbed with the rank of captain, remaining on the army reserve list. Recalled in 1939, he departed for France as part of the BEF. However, he was not one of those who was evacuated at the 'miracle of Dunkirk'; instead he was again wounded and captured at Rouen. Along with thousands of other POWs, he trekked 350 miles from Normandy to Trier in Germany. The Abwehr (German Intelligence) established an 'Irish' POW camp at Friesack and made efforts to win Irish recruits from among the inmates so that they might undertake anti-British espionage and sabotage. Having won a field promotion to major – so now regarded as a senior officer – McGrath appealed to the Germans. The Germans were looking for a senior British officer to help them oversee captured British servicemen with Irish backgrounds in a programmed project to turn them, with the co-operation of IRA personnel, into becoming involved in anti-British activities in Ireland. McGrath fitted the bill, both as an Irish-born officer and one with a Catholic nationalist background. Chosen for these reasons,

McGrath used the role as an opportunity to investigate: masquerading as being motivated and prepared to fight for Ireland against Britain, while, at the same time, winning the prisoners' confidence and conspiring with them to frustrate the Germans' plans. In the event, few collaborated – the men were motivated only by promises of better food and recreation, undertaking the training only to see whether it presented an opportunity for future freedom and survival. The Germans, realising that the project was unlikely to bear fruit, abandoned such efforts. Following this, McGrath encountered, among others, four Irishmen who, along with him, would become part of the Prominenten group. Tom Wall's *Dachau to the Dolomites: The Untold Story of the Irishmen, Himmler's Special Prisoners and the End of WWII* (2019) relates this intriguing but little-known story.

The living nightmare of the death camps and death marches – the widespread disease and starvation; the medical experimentation; the torture and maltreatment; the gas chambers and crematoria – were laid brutally bare. This all impacted hugely on public opinion, both in the western and wider world, and also greatly influenced its leaders. Photographs and newsreel footage reinforced the extreme and extensive disgust toward the Nazi regime as people struggled to come to terms with the unimaginable levels of inhumanity that were engaged in.

8

FIGHTING TO THE FINISH

On 12 April 1945, US President Franklin D. Roosevelt unexpectedly died of a cerebral haemorrhage. On 13 April, Vienna, the capital of Austria, fell to the Russians, and on 16 April, twenty-eight miles east of Berlin, the Russian offensive over the Oder River began. At 4 a.m., three red flares were fired into the darkness over the area of the Küstrin bridgehead – the signal for night to be turned to day by the sudden switching-on of a powerful concentration of bright anti-aircraft searchlights. The searchlights were focused directly ahead, on to the German position, revealing their defences. Next, three green flares were fired and the mightiest artillery barrage ever witnessed along the eastern front erupted – over twenty-thousand massed guns of all calibres unleashed an enormous volume of fire power, slamming forcefully into targets and onto terrain held by the German defenders. The disruption was immense. The main purpose, however, was to kill, lay waste and wreak havoc. The bursting shells mercilessly destroyed all within their danger zones; the enormous detonations blew apart everything and everyone within range. Forests, fields and farmsteads, crossroads and villages, trench dugouts and concrete strongpoints, were flattened – huge craters, widespread fires and heaps of rubble resulted.

The ruinous devastation was accompanied by the thunderously loud tumult of the firing of the guns. The roar from the gun line was resounding and raucous – an unending, reverberating, deafening clamour. It was the unmistakable sound of vast military might in action. To see, hear and experience it caused utter fear. Suddenly, abruptly, it was over. The attacking troops surged forward; it was an eager assault with a venomously murderous and grim intent.

The Germans were, in April 1945, facing huge forces arrayed against them – a calamity of their own making. In the east, the daunting prospect of an immensely superior Soviet offensive was expected. The ratio of forces was overwhelmingly in favour of the Russians. They had swarmed across eastern Europe, having raced headlong for the banks of the Oder River. They outnumbered the Germans significantly: eleven to one in infantry, twenty to one in aircraft and artillery, and seven to one in tanks. The Germans, following defeat after defeat, were ill-prepared for the battle that they knew was about to unfold. The German generals knew that to fight this fight was futile, but an enraged Hitler was vehement in his refusal to surrender. A fierce and bitter struggle, however pointless, was set to be fought; if, as was likely, the battle was lost, it would only bring death and destruction to the German capital and its occupants. Along with this thought of offering a useless and costly defence, foremost in the minds of the German generals was that the Russians thought not only of victory, but of revenge: retaliation for the wrongs, rapes and atrocities committed by the German troops against the Russian population during Operation Barbarossa (the German invasion of Russia) and, of course, for the evidence of genocide recently observed in the newly discovered death camps, with many Russian Jews among the dead. While the Berliners had a vague fearfulness of the consequences of the Russian advance, they did not completely grasp or appreciate the full and dire implications of what was coming.

The great river obstacles – the Rhine to the west and the Oder to the east – were natural barriers to the interior two-thirds of the German landmass. However, the Rhine River had already been successfully breached by the Allies, and they were daily advancing eastwards. The Russians were sweeping westwards and fast-approaching the Oder River. German cities were being bombed day and night. The merciless battle for Berlin was about to begin.

William Robert McClintoch Bunbury, from County Carlow, known, rather oddly, as 'Major the Lord Rathdonnell', was commander of B-Squadron 15th/19th King's Royal Hussars – a tank unit. He was a part of the Allied push eastwards. He and his tank unit had been involved in prior actions in Operation Market Garden; they had slogged through Belgium, fighting fierce and brilliant Nazi resistance, and later fought with forward elements in the Scheldt estuary in order to open the port of Antwerp to Allied shipping. At one stage, in close country with lots of marsh and short fields of view – treacherous going for tanks – he and his Cromwell tank crew had a close call. When bursting through a hedgerow into a lane, they found themselves sixty yards from a German Jagdpanzer IV, the barrel of which had now swung around to point straight at them. He issued a quick-fire order to his gunner, but no shot resulted. The gun had jammed and they were now at the mercy of the Germans; the Germans fired and miraculously missed. Beating an immediate retreat, they next encountered a German with a Panzerfaust who also fired. His shot struck the Cromwell but no real damage resulted.

On 12 April 1945, now in Germany and pushing hard on to the Aller River, McClintoch Bunbury and his crew were involved in a curious event which showed the utter confusion that beset the Wehrmacht during their desperate fighting withdrawal. The local German commander approached the 11th Armoured – of which B-Squadron 15th/19th King's Royal Hussars was a part – under a white flag to ask for a temporary ceasefire. He told them that some miles to the north was an internment camp containing 60,000 political and criminal prisoners. Typhus had broken out in the camp and there was a very real danger that, if the British division continued on its presumed axis, the prisoners would escape and spread the dreaded disease over a wider area. The German commander added that, of course, the Wehrmacht had known nothing about the camp; it was run by the SS at an obscure railhead called Belsen (this, of course, was Bergen-Belsen, the Nazi concentration camp in Lüneburg Heath). Would the British allow the local German forces to disengage and withdraw well north of the camp? In return, the division would be able to take the crossings over the River Aller at Winsen unopposed.

In the event, the precise terms could not be agreed, and this was to cost the regiment dearly. On 13 and 14 April, they had to fight their hardest battle of the war to win those same crossings. The attacks were supported by 1st Battalion, the Cheshire Regiment, and rocket-firing Typhoon aircraft. It was close-quarter battle again – this time against determined and skilled opposition, including German marines. McClintoch Bunbury won the Military Cross (MC) for his part in directing the battle on the first day. By nightfall on 14 April, the town had been taken at a cost of six lives with sixteen more badly wounded. McClintoch Bunbury survived the war but was to die of a brain tumour in 1959, at 44 years of age.

The two Irishmen who fought with the Germans, James Brady and Frank Stringer, have previously been mentioned – besides their involvement in Lieutenant Colonel Otto Skorzeny's military unit, they also became involved in the savage ferocity of the fighting for Berlin. Remarkably, there was also an Irishman on the other side, with the Russians. Sean O'Donovan, the escape artist and brother of Fred, had been captured a number of times by the Germans and escaped from them just as often. While working for a rubble-clearing POW detail, he took an opportunity to abscond amidst confusion caused by two Russian fighter aircraft. With pandemonium ongoing around him, he decided to make a break for it and simply, audaciously, walked away unnoticed. A number of days later, in a shell-shattered copse northwest of Berlin, he was noticed by a band of men: a group of twenty Russian Cossacks on horseback. Brandishing Thompson machine guns, they were not riding on sleek, slender cavalry mounts, but unspectacular, short and shaggy animals more like ponies. Their leader was also armed with a sword; he was ex-navy, and, as a merchant seaman in a previous existence, had been to Dublin. Once it was safely established who Sean O'Donovan was, he and the Cossack leader, 'Thomas', sang the First World War favourite, 'It's a Long Way to Tipperary'. Sean was given a pony with a bloodstained saddle and resumed active warfighting, riding with the Cossacks. It was on horseback that he entered Berlin, having shared in the Cossacks' meagre supplies of vodka and food for a week. Handed over to the Allies, O'Donovan was sent to hospital in England, having endured three years of undernourishment. When he successfully recuperated, he stayed on in the British army, only retiring after a full, long and distinguished career as a regimental sergeant major.

The Third Reich was crumbling, and Frank Stringer and James Brady were on the wrong side – the losing side. One month previously, in mid-March, they found themselves on the wrong side, quite literally. They were on the east side of the Oder River, at the Zehden bridgehead, north of the Küstrin salient. Here, and all along the river bank, the Russians had begun preliminary probing attacks in order to prepare themselves for the coming river-crossing assault. Not only were Stringer and Brady on the wrong side, the bridge which was to see the safe retreat of their unit, No. 1 Company of Jagdverband Mitte, had inadvertently been destroyed.

They set up defensive positions in the north of the bridgehead, which was originally four kilometres wide and the same distance in depth. In the subsequent exchanges, this was to expand and contract, as ground was gained and lost. During the fighting, Brady was slightly wounded and taken across to the far bank and beyond; once recovered, he returned. They could hear the heavy Russian artillery bombardments accompanying the infantry and armour attacks further south at Küstrin, as the Russians seized the bridgehead there. Soon thereafter, the Russians came for theirs at Zehden. Now in late March, Russian shells poured in as the ground was contested, and their position was all the while becoming less and less tenable. Constantly withdrawing to their rear, the size of the defended salient ever shrinking, the casualty count increasing, Brady was again to find himself counted among the wounded, receiving a slight injury to his head; however, it was sufficient enough to see him withdrawn, once again, from the firing line back over the river. The defence virtually collapsed. Those that could, Frank Stringer among them, swam to the far shore for safety.

While Brady recovered, Otto Skorzeny, who had actually seen little of the engagement, travelled to the Austrian Alps to assist in the establishment of the so-called Alpine Fortress. It is believed Frank Stringer was among the group that Skorzeny took with him.

Terrain, troops and time were the three principal considerations in the mind of Colonel General Gotthard Heinrici when he was appointed to ready Army Group Vistula to face the imminent Russian onslaught on the Oder River front. Not wanting to be in charge when the collapse came, and having already displayed his lack of operational field experience, Reichsführer Heinrich Himmler was only too happy to leave. Heinrici had to make do with what forces he had taken over and apply himself to make something substantial out of the insubstantial – to make a defence with his 'ghost armies'. Along the northern half of his 175-mile front he had the 3rd Panzer Army under General Hasso von Manteuffel; along the southern half he had the 9th Army under General Theodor Busse. Just like an apparition, the divisions were an eerie, faint trace of their former strengths – for them, this reality was disastrously scary. They were divisions in name only: makeshift remnants; some soldiers thrown together in a 'Gruppe' whose fighting calibre had long ago expended. Supplemented by the Volkssturm, a militia raised in the last months of the war from teenagers and elderly men, and reservists, they were ill-trained and poorly armed; they brought little combat capability to the defensive effort. Berlin was definitely endangered, and even though they knew this to be true, the Third Reich cabinet found the evidence difficult to accept, with Hitler issuing increasingly unrealistic orders to imaginary full-strength units of troops. Nonetheless, for Colonel General Heinrici the great Soviet offensive was very real and it was expected to arrive shortly, and his new 'command' was the first line it would encounter.

Despite the discouraging state of affairs – the insurmountable difficulties, crippling shortages and ominous inadequacies – Heinrici had to, here and now, somehow render it capable of standing fast. He set about making alterations to the German defence line: he adapted the use of anti-aircraft guns as field guns set in concrete, sited tactically along, and throughout, his line; he added secondary defensive positions 8km to the rear, into which, the night before the Russian attack, he cleverly and covertly withdrew his troops. The latter manoeuvre allowed them to avoid the worst of the massive Russian artillery bombardment, keeping their defensive line intact in order to meet the Russian assault head-on – which they did to good effect, halting it in its tracks. The Seelow Heights, on which he had positioned his defensive line, was a crescent-shaped ridge of high ground overlooking the marshy low-lying western banks of the River Oder; the banks of the Oder were riddled with irrigation canals, over which the assaulting Russian troops and tanks had great difficulty advancing – especially as these obstacles were covered by a point-blank blaze of continuous German fires. Heinrici realised this stiff and unyielding resistance could stall the Russian attack but, ultimately, would not stop it; the sheer weight of their forces would have to tell eventually. He could, however, buy Berlin time to better organise its defences.

Politics, it has been said, is war by other means. The Russians, having endured and survived the German threat of conquest, now characterised the opposite dynamic, using war as politics by other means. Prior to this, in Poland, Stalin had encouraged the 'Home Army' in the Warsaw ghettoes to rise against the German occupiers, thereby implying support. When they did, he offered none, instead sitting back and watching them get slaughtered by the Germans and, in the process, removing any Polish pro-western community. His treacherous strategy cleared the way for a pro-communist Poland after the war, which could act as a buffer zone between Russia and Germany. Despite Stalin reaching an agreement with Churchill and Roosevelt in Yalta in February 1945 as to how the Allies proposed to occupy and partition post-war Germany, he strongly suspected that a secret deal (which was non-existent) had been struck between the Allies and Germany to weigh its defences against the Russians, thereby slowing the Russians' advance and permitting the British and Americans to reach Berlin first. Stalin was therefore insistent that his generals, marshals Zhukov, Koniev and Rokossovski, would spare neither effort nor delay in smashing through the weak defensive line of a disintegrating German army. The competition, especially between Zhukov and Koniev in being the first to reach Berlin, was intense – a rivalry encouraged by Stalin. It was Marshal Zhukov's troops who were being held up by Heinrici's; Marshal Koniev's troops, further south, successfully crossed the Neisse River, making ground westwards, hopeful that Stalin would allow him to swing northwards towards Berlin. Marshal Zhukov, held up and enraged, changed tactics, ordering in his bomber aircraft to concentrate on the enemy guns while his artillery bombed the Seelow Heights and, for good measure, his full tank force joined the assault as well. The German line bucked and broke once resources – essentials like sufficient ammunition, tanks, infantry reinforcements, air cover and fuel – were depleted. The Russians were on their way to Berlin, where James Brady was among the city's defenders awaiting their arrival.

Short-handled shovels, knives, grenades, submachine guns, pickaxes, and extra ammunition were essential; specially adapted drills, tactics and techniques were crucial; more troops and more time were needed; higher casualty rates, along with increased expenditures of ammunition, were expected. This was what the Germans called 'the war of the rats'; this was what fighting in built-up urban terrain – cities like Stalingrad and Berlin – required. Fighting room-to-room in buildings, along streetscapes, and through cities involved assaults from above, at and below ground level: moving through 'mouseholes' (holes breached through interior walls), down trap doors into basements, cellars and even stinking sewers, or confronting the enemy on an upper stairwell or floor. The notion of distance changed as the concept of 'the front' altered. The new reality was one in which the enemy was in front, above, below and behind them all at once – hidden in the rubble, concealed in the ruins, constantly changing positions. Snipers, too, were prevalent and highly effective, using, along with the skill of marksmanship, the qualities of patience, determination and self-control. Fighting room-to-room involved speed and aggression – the use of grenades and spraying interiors with submachine gun fires. The confined spaces and restricted fields of fire and observation made it difficult to gain a foothold. Progress hung by a thread, often depending on small unit actions. Conventional platoon and company-level battle procedures were replaced by smaller groups of 'shock troops' that operated in a manner more suitable to this new close-quarter fighting arena. It was frenetic, brutal and bloody; it was fierce and unforgiving.

When pushing the assault forward, the deeper an advance progressed the more difficult it was to maintain resupplies and keep a clear picture of the battle. Civilians, too, were present; the differentiation between combatants and non-combatants was a distinction not easily made, especially in the fog of war and the heat of the moment, and often they were treated as if they were the same. The fighting was savage, cruel and vicious; murderous and barbaric; sometimes involving primitive, untamed hand-to-hand fighting. The destruction, masonry-filled streets restricted access and sometimes limited the use of tanks and larger artillery. The steamrolling effect of the Wehrmacht war machine, which had once put all of Europe under the German jackboot, was no longer able to come into play.

Hitler's vision of a 'Thousand Year Reich' became a nightmare for the German people. It was no longer a matter of an Aryan 'super race' domination, but a matter of survival. Hitler's insatiable ambition had caused the death of millions, the near total destruction of the entire European continent and embroiled the world in a cataclysmic conflict. The war had wasted precious lives, squandered valuable resources and egregiously misled the efforts of a generation, dissipating their potential, prospects and promise.

Frank Stringer was safely south. He was involved with Lieutenant Colonel Otto Skorzeny's supposed efforts to bring about the Alpine redoubt – the fanciful, even fantastical 'Alpine Fortress' facility for the still-fanatical Führer, who envisioned that up to twenty German divisions would retreat into its defences and continue to fight from there. Despite so much reporting of its suspected existence in Allied intelligence estimates, it was an utter fantasy, never to become fact. Whatever about working to establish a far-fetched Alpine redoubt, James Brady's fate was far less favourable than Stringer's; he grappled directly with the harsh, harrowing harvest of Russian hate, now pitilessly manifest in the maelstrom and mayhem taking place in Berlin. Berliners knew the Russians were coming but they did not believe they were actually going to arrive; the Wehrmacht knew the battle was coming, but they did not realise it was actually winnable. Hitler knew defeat was coming, but he did not believe it was actually going to happen. This twilight between doubt and knowing, between denial and truth, and between certainty and disbelief, prolonged the suffering of the German people. To hold lives to ransom for a brief extension of the Third Reich's existence was an obscenity. The Russians had arrived, the battle was being fought and lost, Hitler was being defeated and the Berliners were to suffer horribly!

Brady's strange and startling reality was that he was now fighting for his life – fighting to keep from being one of the slaughtered. This time he just might not secure his survival. The urban warfare of the Berlin battlefield was a harrowing and perilous actuality; every moment was bewilderingly touch and go – a dreadfully distressing drama between life and death. Brady was wounded in both legs, but survived the savagery of the Berlin battle.

Another Irishman had to leave Ireland in a hurry. Suspected of being an informer, he fled in fear of an IRA assassination attempt. Then, fearing internment for being a member of the pro-Nazi British Union of Fascists, he, at similar speeds, had to leave Britain. He later tried to leave Germany ahead of being arrested for treason, having backed the wrong horse as a broadcaster for the Nazi's English-language propaganda radio programme, *Germany Calling*. William Joyce, from County Galway, was known as 'Lord Haw Haw'; he was German radio's most prominent English-language speaker. For six years, during the war, he had presented the *Germany Calling* radio broadcast programme to audiences in Great Britain and Ireland. Lord Haw Haw had consciously cultivated a characteristic and conceited hallmark broadcasting style, making his one of the most distinctive voices beamed over the radio waves. Joyce was American-born, and Galway-reared and educated.

His father Michael was a successful business man from Ballinrobe, County Mayo; his mother was English. Joyce's broadcasts were much listened to, his audience deriving amusement from his insidious insinuations and heavily slanted, sly style. Contemporaneous records of his broadcasts, transcribed by the BBC, are available at the Imperial War Museum, London, and sound recordings of some of his transmissions, including one of his most famous – his 'goodbye' broadcast on 30 April 1945 – survive. He, however, did not. When he was captured in a chance encounter near the Danish border after a British officer recognised his trademark voice, he ended up being shot four times in the buttocks. Imprisoned in Wandsworth prison in England, he stood trial for treason and, in 1946, became the last man hanged for the offence. In accordance with his wishes, his daughter, Heather Iandalo, succeeded in having his remains returned to Ireland for reburial. He was buried at Bohermore cemetery in Galway on 19 August 1976, thirty years after the hanging.

The day after Lord Haw Haw transmitted his 'farewell' broadcast, Hitler ended his own life in his underground Führerbunker near the Reich Chancellery. The last battle of the European war was over. Germany was defeated, Fascism was vanquished, evil was crushed, democracy was defended. Freedom was won – hard won.

9

AFTERMATH

In late September 2019, a newly built pedestrian bridge was officially opened by the Lord Mayor of Cork, Councillor John Sheehan. The previous February it had been decided by Cork City Council to name the bridge after Ballintemple-born Mary Elmes, in recognition of her role in saving 200 Jewish children from being sent to the death camps. It was the citizens of Cork who first proposed naming the bridge after Mary Elmes so that she may be honoured in her native Cork; as the Lord Mayor said, it was 'hoped that naming the bridge after her would prompt people to delve into her remarkable story'. She worked as a nurse during the Spanish Civil War and later fled to France, where she saved the Jewish children from the death camps. Two of them, Charlotte Berger-Greneche and Georges Koltein, travelled to Cork to witness the woman who saved them being honoured by her native city.

Nor was she the only Irish person to display their unstinting courage and deep compassion. Kilkenny man Hubert Butler operated on his own initiative and travelled extensively in Eastern Europe. Prior to the rise of Hitler, Butler, who spoke Serbo-Croat, worked closely with the Quakers to get dozens of Jews out of Vienna before they were rounded up by the Nazis. A gardener, he had, however, a somewhat suave manner which assisted him in gaining entry to numerous embassies; once there, he solicited visas for those he was hoping to save and managed to get a lot of them out of Vienna, when they otherwise might have died. He even went beyond that, taking illegal risks in moving people out of Austria to Ireland via England; his wife Peggy met them and illegally took them to Bennettsbridge, their Kilkenny home, arranging their onward journeys from there.

A wartime Rome-based priest, Monsignor Hugh O'Flaherty from Killarney, County Kerry, operated a clandestine escape route from his room in the Teutonic (German) college in the Vatican during the Nazi occupation of the Eternal City; it has been estimated that this was instrumental in saving the lives of no fewer than 6,500 Allied prisoners of war, Jewish refugees and members of the Italian anti-fascist resistance. His heroism and humanity was recognised after the war when US Lieutenant General John C.H. Lee presented the US Medal of Freedom to Monsignor O'Flaherty in 1946.

Esther Steinberg was the only known Irish Jewish person (along with her son Leon) to be murdered in the Holocaust until recent research by Dr David Jackson, a consultant statistician, uncovered, according to media reports, three more names: Isaac Shishi, Ephraim Saks and Lena Saks (Ephraim's sister). They were all born in Ireland, but their families returned to Europe when they were children. Together with their families, they were murdered by the Nazis in the Holocaust.

Definitely not forgotten are the 5,000 serving Irish soldiers who swapped uniforms to fight for the British against Hitler, though they were not treated with such deference at the time. Their names were placed on an official, confidential 'blacklist', whereby they were neither welcomed back to Ireland nor could get government public service or local authority jobs. Among these men was Phil Farrington, who took part in the D-Day landings and later was involved in the liberation of Bergen-Belsen concentration camp. Another was John Stout, who was with the Irish Guards as they advanced in a brave, albeit unsuccessful, attempt to capture the key bridge at Arnhem, and who later fought at the Battle of the Bulge, ending the war as a commando.

At its peak during the Second World War, the Irish Defence Forces included some 42,000 serving personnel. During that time, 4,983 people deserted the Irish Defence Forces to join the Allied armies fighting Germany and Japan. The Irish Minister for Defence, Alan Shatter, in a statement to the Dáil in mid-June 2012, announced there would be a pardon and amnesty for soldiers who deserted the Irish army to fight for the Allies during the Second World War. The minister said that, in addressing the question of desertion during this period, the government acknowledged that the Second World War gave rise to circumstances that were grave and exceptional – that no distinction was made between those who fought on the Allied side for freedom and democracy and those who absented themselves for other reasons. The minister, on behalf of the Irish government, apologised for the manner in which these soldiers were treated by the State after the war. At the time of his announcement, it was estimated that 100 'deserters' were still alive. The 2012 announcement of governmental intent to bring forward future legislation that granted them pardon and amnesty recognised the value and importance of their military contribution to the Allied victory.

Shatter said the government recognised the value, and the importance to the State, of the essential service given by all those who served in the Irish Defence Forces throughout the period of the Second World War. It is essential to the national interest that members of the Irish Defence Forces do not abandon their duties at any time, especially at a time of crisis, and no responsible government could ever depart from this principle. Shatter noted that, in August 1945, the government, through an emergency powers order, dealt with those who absented themselves during the war by summarily dismissing them from the Defence Forces and disqualifying them, for seven years, from holding employment or office remunerated by the State's Central Fund; he also pointing out that individuals were not given a chance to explain their absence. Members of the Irish Defence Forces left their posts at that time to fight on the Allied side against tyranny and, together with many thousands of other Irish men and women, played an important role in defending freedom and democracy. Those who fought on the Allied side also contributed to protecting the State's sovereignty and independence, and its democratic values. The minister went on to say that

> in the time since the outbreak of the Second World War our understanding of history has matured. we can re-evaluate actions taken long ago, free from the constraints that bound those directly involved and without questioning or revisiting their motivations. It is time for understanding and forgiveness. At a time of greater understanding of the shared history and experiences of Ireland and Britain, it is right that the role played by Irish veterans who fought on the Allied side be

recognised and the rejection they experienced be understood. To that end, this Government has now resolved to provide a legal mechanism that will provide an amnesty to those who absented themselves from our Defence Forces and fought with the Allied Forces in World War II and to provide a pardon to those who were individually court-martialled. This will be achieved without undermining the general principle regarding desertion. The proposed legislation, which I intend to introduce later this year, will provide that the pardon and amnesty does not give rise to any right or entitlement or to any liability on the part of the State.

However, Shatter emphasised that the government did not condone desertion and 'fully recognises, values and respects the contribution of all those who stood by their post with the Irish Defence Forces'.

It was to emerge, both leading up to and after Victory in Europe Day, 8 May 1945, that there was active, even intense competition between the Allies and the Russians in seeking out German scientists and sending them to work on 'military projects' in their respective countries. Patrick James Ness from Michigan, whose mother was Irish (a McAuliffe, likely from north Cork) and whose father was Norwegian, flew four sorties over Normandy on D-Day in his P47 Thunderbolt ('The Jug') with the 81st Fighter Squadron. He was subsequently seconded to the US Office of Strategic Studies, a forerunner to the Central Intelligence Agency (CIA), via US Air Force Intelligence and was one of those tasked to target and track such expert scientists capable of processing uranium. The Manhattan Project in the US, a research and development undertaking on this front, was already at an advanced stage, and the Russians wanted to replicate this research. So chemists and metallurgists were required on both sides, along with equipment and materials, and supplies of heavy water, metallic uranium and uranium oxide. The British also earmarked the leading lights from among the top echelon of German scientists and successfully appointed these academics in supporting their own efforts. The scientists' valuable expertise was designated for particular purposes, and each one taken on board was also one denied to the opposition; their knowledge and experience was to advance and mature the nuclear weapons programmes of the countries for which they worked. To have the bomb was to possess power; the threat of putting such power to use granted prestige, strength and influence. This race for dominance between superpowers was to become known as the Cold War: a global rivalry between the ideologies of democracy and communism.

A US covert operation codenamed 'Paperclip' was initiated, and those responsible for its undertaking sanitised the wartime record of the involvement of a number of Nazi scientists, reclassifying them with a simple refugee status, thus allowing them to become part of the influx of those entering the US and to work without undue notice. Their previous wartime work – experience and expertise in the areas of specialist research, the development of advanced electronics and rocket propulsion, and chemical and biological innovation – was to become both beneficial and valuable to the modern, sophisticated, forward-looking scientific programmes underway in America.

Much sought after, too, was another classification of German individual – those high-ranking senior SS officers who had succeeded in slipping away amidst the chaos and confusion, evading the clutches of the Allies. Of course, not all of them did; most of the leading members of the defeated Nazi regime were brought to justice and made answerable for their actions. In what were unprecedented and remarkable trials, four judges of the military tribunals set up under the London Charter of 8 August 1945 indicted twenty-four men for crimes against humanity. Nine months of hearings at the Palace of Justice in Nuremberg, from November 1945 to October 1946, were conducted in order for verdicts to be reached. Only three of those on trial were acquitted; the remainder were sentenced to death, life imprisonment or lesser prison terms. Three specially erected scaffolds in the gymnasium of Nuremberg prison saw those twelve men sentenced to death, executed in the early hours of the morning of 17 October 1946. The trials were historic and the extraordinary proceedings were witnessed by two Irish people who had visited the court while it was in session. Thomas Desmond Williams was the first; he was a UCD history graduate, had a position with the British Foreign Office as joint editor for the publication of the archives of its German counterpart, and later, in 1949, he became Professor of Modern History at UCD. The second Irish visitor was the formidable Frances Elizabeth Moran, the first woman Regius Professor of Laws at Trinity College, Dublin.

There were also those Germans who surrendered to the Allies, and one of them was Frank Stringer and James Brady's unit commander, the Austrian lieutenant colonel of the 502nd SS-Jäger Battalion, Otto Skorzeny. He was later to cause much intrigue by arriving in Ireland in 1959 and purchasing Martinstown House and farm in County Kildare, near the Curragh. His journey there began at the war's end, ten days after Hitler committed suicide in the Führerbunker on 30 April 1945, when Skorzeny surrendered to the Americans. He was to stand trial for war crimes in Dachau in 1947, but the case was to collapse and he was acquitted.

Still to face charges from other countries, he was detained but escaped. He went to Madrid and established an import/export agency. He was suspected of being a front organisation, assisting the escape of wanted Nazis from Europe to South America. He was himself to make many trips to Argentina, meeting President Juan Perón and becoming a bodyguard to Perón's wife Eva. Skorzeny supposedly stopped an attempt on her life and was rumoured to have had an affair with her. Six foot, four inches in height and weighing eighteen stone, he had a distinctive scar running along his left cheek, a reminder of a duelling encounter from his student days. Arriving in Ireland for a visit in June 1957, he was to return two years later and take up residence on the Curragh. There were allegations that he had opened up an escape route for ex-Nazis in Spain and that his County Kildare farm was a holding facility, sheltering them, but this claim was unsubstantiated. He was not to be granted permanency of residence in Ireland though, and returned to Madrid, dying of cancer there in 1975. As for his two 'Irish' subordinates, Brady, having participated in clandestine raids, operations and actions, mostly in Romania and later even during the Battle of Berlin, surrendered himself to the British in 1945; brought to London, he was court martialled and received a fifteen-year prison term, which was reduced by three years. Stringer was back in Ireland by the early 1950s but immigrated to Britain soon after. Both were slow, if ever, to mention their wartime experiences.

Like many men of their generation, those returning, especially to southern Ireland, chose not to discuss their experiences. Indeed, many hid their medals and did not broadcast their worthy wartime service fighting the evil Nazi fascist regime. They rarely spoke of it, even to family, their reticence arising from the perception that such service belonged to a non-nationalist narrative and endeavour, and, as a result, was not valued. Their stories have subsequently been written out of the history of their country, not least by themselves. This social and political pressure not to discuss their war service was amplified by the IRA border campaign (1956–62) and the Troubles, which erupted over three decades (1969–98).

With the passage of time and the advantage of perspective came an understanding of the relative importance of the not insignificant contribution made by the Irish during the war: 120,000 men; 70,000 from the 'neutral' south and more than 50,000 from the 'loyal' north. These figures solely account for those that joined the British army. There were others in American, Canadian, New Zealand and Australian uniforms – both native Irish and from the wider Irish diaspora. It is time to excavate them from the corners of Irish history and bring them into the mainstream, albeit complex, heritage of the island of Ireland. It is something to be proud of, and to build on. So let us be proud that we did build on it and help the island develop a positive pluralism – a conscious concession to past history – allowing present inhabitants to better face up to the many future uncertainties and challenges lurking over the horizon.

10

TELLING THE END OF WAR STORY

Sometimes the Hollywood image can become more real than the truth it transmits. What is depicted is often more potent than the actuality it portrays. Yet even the most raw, gritty and hard-edged war film cannot capture combat; it cannot relay the confusion, uncertainty, fear and complexity of the soldiering scenario. A movie implies that a narrative exists, while in conflict the outcome is unpredictable. There is a certain randomness in reality, an arbitrary way in which things unfold, that doesn't suit the film-maker's purpose, for the most part. In cinema, the film-maker's portrayal is what is to be believed. Historical fact is sacrificed to the medium. The product is the priority.

The 1963 epic *The Great Escape*, about the escape of Allied air force prisoners of war, depicts American airmen among the escapees from Stalag Luft III in Zagan, Poland. In actual fact, there were none.

In heightened wartime circumstances, the ordinary is sometimes extraordinary, but there is no audience for this. Joseph Charles 'Big Joe' McCarthy, American with Irish heritage, who flew with the Royal Canadian Air Force, was a member of the famous No. 617 Squadron RAF 'Dam Busters'. He was in the second wave of Lancaster bombers during the 1943 bombing raid, so he was not portrayed – though was mentioned – in the 1955 film *The Dam Busters*, which focused mainly on the first wave that breached the Möhne and Eder dams.

But then there is the argument – and there is merit in it – that however historically imperfect the portrayal of wartime events may be on screen, these movies are responsible for such events becoming more widely regarded than they otherwise might be. However, it is arguable that Gregory Peck's depiction of Monsignor Hugh O'Flaherty in the film *The Scarlet and the Black*, amply demonstrating his bravery and willingness to risk his own life in order to save others, did little to spotlight the real Monsignor from County Kerry; he remained, until recently, largely unknown to people at home and abroad. Huw Wheldon was a wartime comrade and friend of Major Kenneth Donnelly, Royal Ulster Rifles, who was killed at the crossing of the Rhine during Operation Varsity. Wheldon become a well-known producer, author and director at the BBC before becoming its managing director. He also directed the *Epic Battles* series with General Sir Brian Horrocks.

The story of the end of the war has also been told in print, most notably by Irishman Cornelius Ryan in his 1966 book *The Last Battle*. This is one from a trilogy of books about the war. *The Longest Day* (1959) and *A Bridge Too Far* (1974), relating the Allied actions at D-Day and Arnhem respectively, became famous films of the same name. Cornelius Ryan was from Dublin. Born in 1920, he was educated at Synge Street Christian Brothers School and chose journalism as a career, joining *The Daily Telegraph* in London, in 1940, as a war correspondent. He became an American citizen in 1951, having moved to America four years earlier, in 1946, to work with *Time* magazine initially and other publications thereafter. Another Irish war correspondent was Denis Johnston, a BBC war correspondent between 1942 and 1945 whose reports covered the crossing of the Rhine River and who was one of the first to reach Buchenwald concentration camp.

In Field Marshal Bernard Law Montgomery's 1958 autobiography *The Memoirs of Field-Marshal the Viscount Montgomery of Alamein, K.G.*, he wrote an account of the occurrences that he believed were important to impart; he covered the entire duration of the war, but also his life. Following the Eighth Army's victory at El Alamein, Allied Forces pursued the Germans and Italians out of Egypt, through Libya and into Tunisia. On 23 January 1943, the Eighth Army captured Tripoli, the capital of Libya and a vital port. Anti-aircraft defence for Tripoli was provided by 9th Derry HAA Regiment, which received an early visit from then Lieutenant General Montgomery,

Eighth Army Commander. Visiting the gunners of 24 HAA Battery (a sub-unit of 9th HAA Regiment), Monty told them that he too was a Derryman! A controversial figure who was not well liked by US Generals, Montgomery was often ridiculed in Hollywood cinema – often inaccurately shown as an overly cautious, eccentric and vainglorious character. His memoir includes some thoughts on high command during wartime; it is an insightful overview from someone who knows about the hard lessons of actual warfare.

Audie Murphy was one of the most decorated American combat soldiers of the Second World War, and he was of Irish descent. After the war, he had a successful twenty-one-year career as an actor, even playing himself in the 1955 autobiographical film *To Hell and Back*, based on his 1949 memoir of the same name. It was the biggest film hit for Universal Studios at that time. After his death in a plane crash in 1971, he was interred with full military honours at Arlington National Cemetery; his grave is the second-most-visited grave site after that of President John F. Kennedy, also of Irish descent. His military career was one of constant involvement in small combat actions where courage and soldiering skills were required; he displayed that he had these in abundance, receiving awards, wounds and promotions, and even a field commission. Though not involved in D-Day, he was involved in Operation Dragoon, the invasion of southern France on 15 August 1944. In all, he was involved in forty films, including *The Red Badge of Courage* and *The Unforgiven*, directed by John Huston, who later became an Irish citizen.

Huston himself served in the army, as a captain, from 1942 onwards, making films for the Signal Corps. He made three films that were deemed too controversial and so were not released, or were censored or banned outright. He nonetheless rose to the rank of major and received the Legion of Merit award for 'courageous work under battle conditions'. He was to live and work in Ireland for a while and had an involvement with the Irish film industry, helping to foster a productive environment for Irish film. He was supported by then-Taoiseach Jack Lynch, who, through the Film Act of 1970, encouraged foreign production companies with tax breaks if they shot on location in Ireland. A book by Mark Harris, *Five Came Back: A Story of Hollywood and the Second World War*, focused on John Ford, who, with one of his closest friends, Michael Morris, 3rd Baron Killanin, collaborated on the making of *The Quiet Man*. Interestingly, both Michael

Morris, 79th Armoured Brigade, and his wife (Mary) Sheila Cathcart Dunlop from Oughterard, County Galway, were awarded MBEs; she, for her work contributing towards breaking wartime German codes; he, for his work with Hobart's Funnies – the range of modified tanks operated by the 79th. Frank Capra, George Stevens and William Wyler were all involved in the war effort.

Sir Freddy Pile, General Officer Commanding Anti-Aircraft Command, a position he held throughout the war, was the only British general to retain the same command throughout the entire war. He tells his wartime tale in the book *Ack-Ack: Britain's Defence Against an Air Attack During the Second World War*. His father was Lord Mayor of Dublin (1900–01) and his son, Frederick Devereux Pile, served as a major (later colonel) in the Royal Tank Regiment, winning the MC during the British army's advance into Germany in 1945.

Films, books, memorials, memoirs, unit histories, diaries, letters, museum displays, all tell the tale of the end of the war. The many versions told require a filter in order to decipher fact from fiction – exaggeration from what is accurate – so that one might interpret the deeds recorded with an appreciation for the service and sacrifice rendered, which secured freedom against encroaching tyranny.

A CHRONOLOGY OF THE END OF THE SECOND WORLD WAR

December 1943	General Montgomery reviews the 'COSSAC plan' and throughout early January 1944 he revises and expands it.
January 1944	General Eisenhower approves Monty's revised plan and it becomes the SHAEF plan – five beaches are to be invaded instead of three and an extra airborne division is to land at H-hour.
3 June 1944	D-Day is postponed from 5 June to 6 June due to weather information received from Ireland.
5–6 June 1944	Operation Neptune commences: the marshalling and organisation of over 6,000 ships tasked with getting the invasion troops across the English Channel and to shore.
6 June 1944	Prior to H-hour, airborne landings are conducted to secure critical objectives and protect the flanks of the invasion force on shore against counter-attacks. D-Day: Allied troops land on five Normandy beaches; surprise is achieved and, at the end of the day, a lodgement has been successfully achieved. The second front is opened.
8 June 1944	The US First Army and British Second Army link up at Port-en-Bessin.
12 June 1944	Utah and Omaha beachheads are joined up.

13 June 1944	The V-1 (Vengeance) rocket offensive against London commences.
18 June 1944	The 'Great Storm' off the Normandy coastline commences and lasts for three days. It destroys two Mulberry harbours; thereafter only the British Mulberry at Arromanches is useable.
22 June 1944	Operation Bagration, the Russian summer offensive, commences, destroying the German Army Group Centre and completely rupturing the German front line.
27 June 1944	Following a combined land-and-sea bombardment, US Forces take Cherbourg.
29 June 1944	Operation Epsom, to recapture Hill 112 southwest of Caen, is unsuccessful.
4 July 1944	The Canadians attempt to take the western approaches to Caen in Operation Windsor. The raid is only partially successful.
8 July 1944	Operation Charnwood, the British attempt to capture Caen, gets underway. A combined British–Canadian offensive seizes it two days later.
17 July 1944	Rommel's car is strafed by two Canadian Spitfires from 412 Squadron. He receives a head injury and is hospitalised. It is to be the end of his army career.
18 July 1944	Operation Goodwood commences east of Caen and the US First Army takes Saint-Lô.
20 July 1944	An assassination attempt is made against Adolf Hitler inside his Wolf's Lair field headquarters near Rastenburg, East Prussia. He survives.
25 July 1944	Operation Cobra commences: the US First Army attempts to spring troops out west of Saint-Lô through the German defences.
30 July 1944	Operation Bluecoat is launched by the British, southeast of Caumont, to secure the road junction of Vire and the high ground of Mont Pinçon. Operationally, the attack was planned to exploit the success of Operation Cobra.

8 August 1944	Canadians launch Operation Totalise, moving southwards towards Falaise; it ends two days later.
14 August 1944	Allies launch Operation Tractable in an attempt to encircle the fleeing Germans in the Falaise Pocket.
15 August 1944	Operation Dragoon (initially Operation Anvil) gets underway and the Allies land in the south of France (Marseilles).
21 August 1944	The Falaise Pocket is sealed, with around 50,000 German troops trapped inside.
25 August 1944	The German garrison surrenders the French capital, completing the liberation of Paris.
September 1944	The rapid advance in Europe results in supply and fuel resupply difficulties being experienced by the Allies.
1 September 1944	General Eisenhower assumes direct command of Allied Ground Forces from Montgomery, who is promoted to field marshal.
3 September 1944	The Allies enter Brussels.
8 September 1944	The first V-2 (Vengeance) rockets fall on London.
10 September 1944	Operation Comet, an Allied plan to land over the Nederrijn River near Arnhem and seize crossing points, is cancelled.
15 September 1944	The French government issues arrest warrants for Philippe Petain and members of his Vichy Cabinet.
17 September 1944	Operation Market Garden is launched – the aim is to seize a series of bridges that could provide an Allied invasion route into Germany. The Allies overstretch themselves and, after nine days, the operation fails to secure the furthest, and most vital, bridge at Arnhem (approximately 300 Irishmen are involved).
30 September 1944	Calais is retaken by the Allies; Canadian troops advance west and north of Antwerp.
8 October 1944	German forces are now fighting on their own country's border.

9 October 1944	The Fourth Moscow Conference, a meeting between Stalin and Churchill, commences; it is regarding the future of Eastern Europe.
13 October 1944	The Germans launch V-1 and V-2 rockets against Antwerp to hinder the Allies' use of the port.
18 October 1944	The Volkssturm is founded; it recruits young boys and elderly men to defend the German fatherland.
November 1944	German V-2 rockets launched from mobile vehicles are proving effective; the only way to defeat them is to capture the terrain and routes from where they are launched.
8 November 1944	The Allies take the island of Walcheren; British minesweepers clear the approaches to Antwerp port, which proves essential in supplying the Allied push into Germany.
15 November 1944	Russian forces are thirty miles from Budapest on the Eastern Front.
27 November 1944	The first time the RAF use Tallboy bombs over Berlin.
16 December 1944	The Germans mount a hugely ambitious, initially successful surprise counterattack in the Ardennes. The Battle of the Bulge commences. Driving into the centre of the Allied line, Hitler hopes to separate the British and American armies, and strike towards and recapture the port of Antwerp. This last throw of the dice commits the Wehrmacht's strategic reserve, troops and combat capabilities, which otherwise could have been deployed on the Eastern Front against the advancing Russians.
19 December 1944	The towns of St Vith and Bastogne, important road hubs and junctions, are under threat; hurriedly reinforced, they hold out, are bypassed and become surrounded. The German advance continues.
22 December 1944	St Vith falls to the Germans.

24 December 1944	Clearer weather allows Allied air supremacy to take effect; the German advance is bombed and isolated forward units and supplied by air drops.
1 January 1945	A surprise sudden attack by the German Luftwaffe in Operation Bodenplatte catches Allied airfields in Holland, Belgium and Northern France unawares, destroying hundreds of aircraft on the ground. The Allies react and inflict such serious losses on their attackers that they effectively put the Luftwaffe out of action for the remainder of the war.
2 January 1945	The Allied counter-attack in the Ardennes begins to gain momentum. Hitler refuses to accede to requests from his generals to withdraw German troops back to Germany.
17 January 1945	Warsaw falls to the Russians.
24 January 1945	Army Group Vistula is formed to defend Germany's Eastern Front from the advancing Russian army.
27 January 1945	German forces are made to retreat from all territories taken in their advance in the Ardennes; the bulge is eliminated.
3 February 1945	Berlin suffers its worst air raid of the war at the hands of Allied bombers.
4 February 1945	The Yalta Conference between Stalin, Roosevelt and Churchill determines the shape of post-war Germany.
13 February 1945	Budapest falls to the Russians.
18 February 1945	The Allies break through the Westwall (the Siegfried Line).
7 March 1945	The Allies cross the Rhine River over the damaged Ludendorff Bridge at Remagen before it can be completely destroyed by the retreating Germans. Subsequent German attempts to destroy it are a failure, until it collapses of itself.
22 March 1945	An audacious attempt by some US Allied troops to cross the Rhine has a favourable outcome and a bridgehead is established at Oppenheim.

23 March 1945	Operation Plunder and Operation Varsity are launched by the 21st Army Group under Field Marshal Montgomery; it sees the Allies cross the Rhine in strength, south of Wesel, after a planned large-scale attack using both ground and airborne troops.
28 March 1945	It becomes apparent that General Eisenhower no longer considers Berlin a strategic military target; it is much to the annoyance of the British, who feel a position of strength in post-war politics has been foregone.
April 1945	Advancing Allied troops begin to discover the unimaginable horrors of German concentration camps, already witnessed by the Russians while advancing through Poland.
1 April 1945	The US Allied armies link up and the Ruhr Pocket is closed.
4 April 1945	Bratislava falls to the Russians.
12 April 1945	US President Franklin D. Roosevelt dies unexpectedly. Vice President Harry S. Truman is made president.
15 April 1945	Arnhem is liberated by Canadian forces.
16 April 1945	The Battle for Berlin begins along the Oder River.
21 April 1945	Russian troops enter the outskirts of Berlin.
30 April 1945	Adolf Hitler commits suicide, by gunshot, in his Führerbunker.
8 May 1945	Following the formal acceptance by the Allies of the unconditional surrender of Nazi Germany's armed forces, Victory in Europe Day is declared.

TIMELINE: OPERATION VARSITY AND PLUNDER

23 March 1945

1500 Hours   Montgomery sends a message to the men of 21st Army Group:

The enemy thinks he is safe behind this great river obstacle. We all agree that it is a great obstacle, but we will show that enemy that he is far from safe behind it. This great Allied fighting machine, composed of integrated land and air forces, will deal with the problem in no uncertain manner. And having crossed the River Rhine, we will crack about the plains of northern Germany, chasing the enemy from pillar to post. The swifter and more energetic our action, the sooner the war will be over, and that is what we all desire; to get on with the job and finish off the German war as soon as possible. Over the Rhine then, let us go. And good hunting to you all on the other side. May the Lord Almighty in Battle give us victory in this our latest undertaking, as He has done in all our battles since we landed in Normandy on D-Day.

1600 Hours   Montgomery signals the code words 'Two if by Sea' to launch Operation Plunder. A ferocious preliminary artillery bombardment follows against some thousand identified targets on the east bank of the Rhine River, among them enemy command posts, troop concentration areas, strong points, road junctions, artillery locations and anti-aircraft batteries. Thereafter, they were dug in defensive positions on the east bank and suffered a sustained barrage of artillery fire in order to destroy and debilitate enemy defences.

1900 Hours   British assault units proceed to their start lines along the west bank of the Rhine River in readiness for their scheduled crossings.

2200 Hours   51 Highland Division (154 Brigade), using tracked amphibious Buffalos, begin their river crossing towards Rees.

Lead elements of 1st Special Service 'Commando' Brigade begins their attack, taking four minutes to cross the river towards Wesel. Further waves of commandos join them at intervals.

2300 Hours   200 Lancasters from RAF Bomber Command begin an aerial bombardment on the town of Wesel, reducing most of it to ruins.

24 March 1945

0100 Hours   1st Special Service 'Commando' Brigade, having seized the centre of Wesel, begins to dig in among the rubble and ruination.

0200 Hours   15th Scottish Division and 30th US Division attack.

0300 Hours   79th US Division attack.

0400 Hours   21st Army Group establishes itself on the east bank; the bridgehead begins, the initiative created and the momentum now underway. The Allies continue to develop the situation. Operation Plunder had been more of a success than anyone had dared hope.

1000 Hours   Operation Varsity begins in support of Operation Plunder. Airborne troops are inserted. It is the largest airborne operation in history to be conducted on a single day in one location. A part of Operation Plunder, it involves the landing of two airborne divisions after the initial amphibious river crossing; they are only a short distance in front of the advancing troops. A total of 541 transport aircraft and 1,350 gliders, escorted by over 2,000 fighter aircraft, take two-and-a-half hours to insert all the airborne troops. All objectives are achieved and the link-up with elements of the amphibious force take place (15th Scottish Infantry Division join elements of 6th Airborne Division).

2359 Hours   The first Allied brigade is across the Rhine.

27 March

Twelve bridges suitable for carrying the weight of heavy armour are set up across the Rhine. Allies have fourteen divisions on the east bank of the river, penetrating ten miles into German-held territory and establishing a secure bridgehead.

BIBLIOGRAPHY

Ambrose, Stephen E., *Citizen Soldiers* (London: Simon & Schuster, 1997).

Atkinson, Rick, *The Guns at Last Light* (New York: Picador, 2013).

Beevor, Antony, *Berlin: The Downfall 1945* (London: Viking, 2002).

Blake Knox, David, *Hitler's Irish Slave* (Dublin: New Ireland Books, 2014).

Clark, Lloyd, *Crossing the Rhine* (New York: Atlantic Monthly Press, 2008).

Felton, Mark, *Castle of the Eagles* (London: Icon Books Ltd., 2017).

Harvey, Dan, *A Bloody Dawn: The Irish at D-Day* (Dublin: Merrion Press, 2019).

Harvey, Dan, *A Bloody Week: The Irish at Arnhem* (Dublin: Merrion Press, 2019).

Kershaw, Ian, *The End: Hitler's Germany 1944–45* (London: Penguin, 2011).

Lewis, Damien, *The Nazi Hunters* (London: Quercus, 2015).

Montgomery, Bernard, *Memoirs of Field-Marshal the Viscount Montgomery of Alamein, K.G.* (London: Collins, 1958).

O'Reilly, Terence, *Hitler's Irishmen* (Cork: Mercier Press, 2008).

Overy, Richard, *The Bombing War: Europe 1939–1945* (London: Allen Lane, 2013).

Ryan, Cornelius, *The Last Battle* (London: Collins 1966).

Wall, Tom, *Dachau to the Dolomites* (Dublin: Merrion Press, 2019).

Whiting, Charles, *Bounce the Rhine* (Kent: Spellmount, 2002).

INDEX

Note: Page references in bold refer to maps.

Index

Index

Index